ACC

M000206043

THE TIME AND PLACE THAT GAVE ME LIFE

An arresting, beautiful, often searing study of humanity during the racially turbulent 1940s, '50s and '60s. Peers inside the straight lines of a history book to where the lives were actually lived and the pain and joy and anger felt. I was seriously moved by [this] book.

~ **Ted Green**, documentary filmmaker

This is more than a memoir. Janet Cheatham Bell has seasoned her personal story with some little-known history of African Americans in Indiana.

~ **Julian Bond** (1940-2015) former Professor, University of Virginia; Board Chairman, NAACP

The Time and Place That gave Me Life should be intentionally placed in public libraries and school media centers, private, public and charter, throughout the state of Indiana. It is a must read because it's about US! It magnificently describes how racism (the glue that holds all the other isms in place) impacts, influences and shapes not only the author's internal and external experiences, but that of others as well. I applaud and am so proud of Janet Cheatham Bell whom I have known and admired for many years.

~ **Patricia Payne**, Director Office for Racial Equity, Indianapolis Public Schools

Here is the best form of social history: This memoir focuses on an ordinary individual but also illuminates the experiences of many over time.

~ **Nancy Gabin**, author
*Feminism in the Labor Movement and
the United Auto Workers, 1933-1975*

Janet Cheatham bell has crafted a compelling memoir about growing up in Indiana.

~ **Monroe Little** in *Indiana Magazine of History*,
December 2008

The Time and Place That Gave Me Life sounds a familiar horn, one that echoes tremendous struggles that blacks in America have endured. Yet it is a refreshing voice speaking to blacks' belief in family, faith, community, and education. A memoir that renders a great service. Bell helps us hope in the ideals of freedom, democracy, progress, self-preservation, and determination.

~ **Valerie Grim**, Chair, African American and
African Diaspora Studies, Indiana University

Mixed Marriage

A MEMOIR

Mixed Marriage

A MEMOIR

JANET CHEATHAM BELL

SABAYT
PUBLICATIONS

80 ❖ ଔ

Mixed Marriage: A Memoir

SABAYT PUBLICATIONS
ISBN 978-09616649-5-4

To contact the author or to purchase copies, please see
www.janetcheathambell.com

Book & cover design by Merridee LaMantia

Belmantia Publishing Services

BelmantiaPublishing@gmail.com

ဆို❖ൠ

MIXED MARRIAGE:
a marriage between people of different
races or religions.

Merriam Webster's Collegiate Dictionary, 11th edition, 2004
(Earliest recorded usage in English, 1699)

*A true soul mate is a mirror, the person who…brings
you to your own attention…. because they tear down
your walls, smack you awake. But to live with a soul
mate forever? Nah. Too painful. Soul mates come into
your life to reveal another layer of yourself to you, and
then they leave.*

from *Eat, Pray, Love* by Elizabeth Gilbert

ဆို❖ൠ

ॐ ✤ ३

This book is dedicated

to Samaiyah, Juno and Asha who continue the family story;
and is for all those who wanted to keep reading
when they reached the end of
The Time and Place That Gave Me Life.

ॐ ✤ ३

Preface

This book continues the story I began in *The Time and Place That Gave Me Life,* published by Indiana University Press in 2007. I intended to include my entire story in that book, but once I started writing, I had more to say than I had anticipated. Not wanting to burden readers with a thick, heavy book, I ended the first part of my memoir as I prepared to leave Indiana, the place that gave me life.

The first installment began with some background on my parents, detailed the events of my childhood, ending when I finished college, a slog that took ten years. While I worked on my degree, I lived through self-doubt, marriage, the death of my three-month-old baby, and divorce. I didn't have a clear career goal, other than avoiding life as a maid, which had been my first paid employment. At the time, domestic work was what most black women did to earn money. I left Indiana because I wanted to be away from the scene of my struggles and grief. I also needed psychic and physical space to discover who I was apart from the expectations of family and all the people who "knew" me. I was in a mood to create a life of my choosing.

As it turns out, holding off on writing this second part of my memoir, was wise. I needed time to process what I was learning as I wrote about the events of my life. For many years, I had avoided facing situations that I found painful or embarrassing. However, I couldn't write honestly about my experiences without carefully examining what had happened. The more time that passes as I process these traumas, the more layers of denial I have been able to peel away. Consequently, I am coming to understand myself better than I ever knew was possible. Being able to confront my anxieties and accept all aspects of who I am, unconditionally, has helped me become more patient with, and less judgmental of other people. In addition, I have achieved a measure of personal serenity.

Despite these benefits of autobiography, I don't expect to write another memoir. Instead, I want to finish a novel I started several years ago. But, who knows, I may change my mind.

I write as I perceived things at the time, which, of course, may not correspond with the views of others present at the same events. I also regularly add a contemporary interpretation of why I think things evolved as they did.

Contents

Chapter 1

Going to War

Racism is in large measure a form of psychological warfare.

~ Johnnetta Cole

Michigan has burly pugnacious winters, unlike the little sissified three-to-four month cold spells in central and southern Indiana. Heavy snowfalls with towering windswept drifts begin early and last well past the calendar's barren proclamation of spring. I distinctly remember a winter when I pulled my boots from the back of the closet in early November and wore them every day until May.

I moved to Saginaw, Michigan for my first job after college. Sam Moore, Principal of MacArthur High School, had traveled to Indiana University's (IU) Education Placement Office to interview me the previous spring, just before I graduated. In that interview, he offered me the position of assistant librarian at MacArthur. And because it was the first offer I'd had that was not in my hometown of Indianapolis, I accepted immediately. I would begin in the fall of 1964.

I was in search of a different life, but had no idea that in Michigan I would meet my next husband, and he would be *white!* The civil rights movement that began in 1954 with the U.S. Supreme Court (SCOTUS) decision in *Brown v. the Board of Education in Topeka*, had initiated lots of changes, but in the mid 1960s, interracial marriages were still rare. The 1960 U.S. Bureau of the Census reported that 99.6 percent of marriages were between people of the same skin color. That percent didn't begin to increase until after 1967, when SCOTUS ruled in *Loving v. Virginia*, that laws forbidding mixed marriages were unconstitutional. Before I tell the story of my mixed marriage, however; I need to set the stage.

I had lingered at IU the summer after I graduated because my space in the rooming house on Fourth Street was the only home I had. My husband and I had split up the previous summer and departed the house we shared, storing our divided furnishings with relatives. When I realized early in the marriage that it was not going to be "happily ever after" as I had expected, I decided to go back home. Mama made it clear, however, that my parent's house was no longer my home. WHAAAAT? The place where I grew up and had lived most of my life was not *home*? Mama would not budge, saying emphatically, "Your place is with your husband."

I could not have felt more abandoned if she had driven me thousands of miles away and left me in an unknown location. Was it even possible not to have a home? I simply couldn't believe it. *I no longer had a home.* Didn't everybody have a home somewhere? If my own mother wouldn't take me in, who would? That rejection and my husband's treating me as if what I wanted to do with my life was irrelevant, catapulted me into the realization that the *only* person I could count on was ME! This painful wisdom forced me to get serious about my college studies, and in June, I received my decree and my degree. I was out of a marriage that had felt like a large stone pulling me underwater, and as an *educated* woman I could take care of myself.

Aside from my years at IU in Bloomington, I had spent my entire life in Indianapolis and couldn't wait to live somewhere else. Life had to be better away from the scene of my agony. If I was nervous about going off by myself, the anticipation of a fresh start more than made up for it. I was moving to a place where I didn't know anybody. Sam who hired me, was the

Me in 1964

only person I had even *met* from Saginaw. Finally, I could live my life without the oversight of a parent or husband, far from events I didn't even want to think about, and absent the people who only pretended to care about me.

After I told my parents I was moving to Saginaw, Mama begged me to accept the offer I'd received from the Indianapolis Public Schools (IPS). But I'd had enough of IPS. After attending a segregated elementary school, being marginalized in an "integrated" high school, then having to fight the system's racist policies in my effort to do student teaching in the school of my choice, I wasn't giving IPS another swipe at me. When that plea didn't work, Mama pulled out her scary bag. "Don't you know how dangerous it is out here for a single woman? What will you do if something happens in a place where you don't know a soul? *Anything* could happen to an unmarried woman running around by herself!"

I was a twenty-seven-year-old divorcée, but as she had done throughout my life, Mama dealt with me as if I were a developmentally delayed ten-year-old. "Ma, you were younger than I am when you left home. You were an unmarried *twenty*-year-old when you came to Indianapolis."

"That was different. I *had* to leave home if I wanted to go to high school. And I stayed with family. It's unheard of for a single woman to go off on her own."

Mama left her home in rural Tennessee in 1926, and it may have been unheard of then for a woman to live alone, but that was exactly what I intended to do. However, I hadn't counted on Daddy's usual resourcefulness. He plugged into the family network looking for connections, and lo and behold, found a cousin in Saginaw. I think Cousin Odahlia Rance was a distant relative of Daddy's mother, but the details hardly mattered. If there was any family relationship it was understood they would take you in when you were new in town. Mama was thrilled. I can't say I was peeved to learn there would be some family in an unfamiliar town; but my determination to live on my own was unchanged. I would stay with the new-found cousins only until I found a place, a couple of weeks at most.

Either in protest, or because she couldn't handle my leaving, Mama decided not to join us on the five-to-six-hour ride north. Daddy picked me up and I loaded his car with my clothes and books. The two of us drove to Saginaw with a stopover in Lansing where we had lots of relatives. Mama's uncle, Maynard Johnson, and all ten of his children and their families lived in Lansing. Most of the men worked in the city's General Motors Fisher Body Plant. I imagine that Daddy stopped in Lansing, not only to visit, but also to let them know I would be living nearby, and to show me that close family was a mere two-hour drive away.

Saginaw in 1964 was a small city of about 98,000 people, more than sixty-five percent of whom were homeowners. It boasted several industries including iron foundries and manufacturers producing everything from corsets and girdles to car steering gears and transmissions. An indication of the city's rapid growth was that two new hospitals had been built since 1950. There was also a significant farming community in the fertile Saginaw River Valley that attracted migrating workers to harvest the beans, wheat and sugar beets. The local sugar factory refined 42,000,000 pounds of sugar annually. The city was served by one daily newspaper, *The Saginaw News*, three radio stations and two television stations. Along with the nearby towns of Bay City and Midland, Saginaw operated the Tri-City Airport.

My Saginaw cousins, the Rances, lived in a comfortable and relatively new home at 345 South Twenty-First Street. Odahlia, her husband Beale, and their three young sons—Kelvin, Ronald, and Jerrold—were a picture-perfect middle-class family. She was a reticent, attractive woman, ten years or so older than me and taught in the city school system. I don't remember if they had an extra bedroom or if they put the boys together and gave me one of their rooms. I was grateful for their hospitality, but knew I wouldn't be there long. Mama hoped I'd be with the Rances long enough to see that I needed to come back home. So far as I was concerned, I would never live in Indianapolis again. Life, however, has a way of calling you on your "never's."

The first thing I had to do was buy a car. The Negro part of town was ten miles from MacArthur and I didn't consider relying on public transportation to get me there every morning. Daddy was the family's car aficionado so I asked him for advice. He said I should finance through a bank rather than the dealer, and to find out how much I could borrow before I negotiated the price of the car. He also offered to co-sign the loan because he knew I had no credit history. Once the bank confirmed that I was employed by the Saginaw Township school system, they didn't hesitate to finance the car. I knew I wanted an inexpensive, but brand-new car—one I could afford, but that was somehow unique. Plymouth had just come out with a new model called a "fastback," the sporty aerodynamically designed Barracuda with a huge tinted rear window. The slanted rear window gave the car a shape that resembled its namesake. I liked the jazzy look and settled on a white one with a gold-colored leather-like interior. Buying my first car without Daddy's help was one more step on my stride to total independence. As I intended, the Barracuda got lots of attention wherever I drove it.

I needed the car not only to drive to work, but also to follow up on leads for a place to live. It was turning out that finding an apartment in Saginaw was as unlikely as finding a wealthy man in prison. For starters, blacks were barred from living on the west side of town where Mac-Arthur was located, and the landlords were not shy about saying so. I found this out when Odahlia told me about a west side rental posted at the Saginaw Board of Education. Martha Ludwick, the woman looking for a renter, told me straight-out she did not rent to Negroes. My cousin was not surprised, but thought it was worth a try. Later, I filed a complaint against Ludwick with the Michigan Civil Rights Commission (CRC). I had no desire to live in a house where the landlady didn't want to rent to black folks, but the formal complaint did some good. In a ruling dated March 15, 1965, the CRC ordered the Saginaw Board of Education to add this statement to their housing listing forms: "I agree to rent on a non-discriminatory basis as indicated by the Michigan Civil Rights Commission policy."

Most Saginaw residences were single-family homes, and there were few apartment complexes; none on the east side where blacks lived. It was beginning to look as if my only option was renting a room in somebody's house— somebody, that is, other than Odahlia and Rance.

Everyone, including Odahlia, called her husband by his last name, Rance. He and his brother were both entrepreneurs. He owned Rance Insurance Agency at 117 South Sixth Street, and his brother owned a furniture store. Odahlia was visibly nervous about having another, younger woman in her house, and took care to know where I was at all times. Although I was embarrassed by her vigilance, I understood where she was coming from. Rance's playful glibness, which no doubt served him well as an insurance salesman, could be interpreted as flirtatious. He was always respectful to me, but undoubtedly, she knew things about him that I didn't. Late one night when Rance was out, Odahlia opened the door to my room, looked in, then closed it again without saying a word. I don't know whether she was expecting to discover him there, or to find me gone.

Most east side rentals were rooms in homes where they needed help paying the mortgage. None of them felt private enough for me; it would have been like moving in with a family. I was as diligent as a squirrel burying nuts for winter, but it was impossible to find an acceptable place. I had been looking for months when Odahlia announced she had found something for me. It was an upstairs apartment, almost, at the Ferrell household at 219

North Ninth Street. Mrs. Rosa Ferrell was a street-smart and financially ambitious woman who sprinkled her conversations with biblical references to display her religious piety. I was told she owned two houses in addition to the one she and her family lived in. For additional income, she was converting the attic of her home into a kitchenette apartment. The conversion was not complete, but she and Odahlia decided that it was far enough along for me to move in.

I was so relieved to see a place with a private entrance that I was willing to put up with the half-done apartment; it was certainly better than renting someone's spare room without even a lock on the door. The almost-apartment was smaller than I would have preferred—I'd have to live, sleep, and eat in a room about ten feet long and four feet wide—but I was more aware of the missing walls. Studs for the kitchen and bathroom walls were there, but the drywall had yet to be attached. The miniature appliances and plumbing were installed in the little kitchen and the bathroom, which was so tiny I couldn't step out of the bathtub without bumping into the sink or toilet. Mrs. Ferrell also had house rules about noise and male visitors; neither was allowed. Did she really believe I'd want visitors with a see-through bathroom? I bought a sofa bed to sleep on, and when the bed was down, I couldn't open the room's only door. I'd had a far grander vision for my first apartment.

Salting the wound of my disappointment was that I had to drive nearly ten miles to get to my job on the west side of Saginaw. Each morning that I grappled with traffic and icy streets, I was reminded that people who looked like me could not live in the township where I worked. Was this Michigan or Mississippi? Michigan's laws didn't *officially* support racial segregation, but whites have always been free to break the law in pursuit of restricting and oppressing black people.

In Saginaw, the Maginot line was the Saginaw River that flowed south out of Saginaw Bay splitting the city into east and west. Originally, when the area was the center of the nation's lumber industry, there had been two different towns, East Saginaw and Saginaw City, on opposite sides of the river; the two towns were combined in 1890. That river became a more effective barrier than the Berlin Wall— many East Berliners managed to get over the wall, but only one black family resided west of the Saginaw River. The Porterfield's, who were light enough to be mistaken for white from a distance, apparently were living on the west side before the black population in Saginaw grew large enough to make whites uneasy. Like many northern industrial cities, Saginaw became adamant about where blacks could and could not live as the Great Migration swelled. After each world war, large numbers of blacks left the South to look for jobs and to escape the harsh and unrelenting racial oppression. Between 1920 and 1930 Saginaw's population grew from 61,903 to 80,715. Only 2,000 more people were added between 1930 and 1940, but another 10,000 came between 1940 and 1950. In the time-honored tradition of American racism, black folks could work wherever they could manage to get hired, but were only allowed to reside in specific, often undesirable, places.

I was particularly insulted by Saginaw's rigid boundary because a year earlier in 1963 in Birmingham, Alabama, black folk had demanded an end to similar apartheid conditions. They stood their ground despite the brutal assaults by Bull Connor's dogs and water cannons. Those vicious attacks on peaceful citizens spurred President Kennedy to send a new civil rights bill to Congress. Kennedy reportedly said, "The civil rights movement should thank God for Bull Connor. He's helped it as much as Abraham Lincoln." The president may have believed in equal rights for all Americans, but he was also trying to save face as "leader of the free world." Other nations were vocal in their outrage that elected public officials in the U.S. could be so brazenly barbaric. Yet, here I was, in a *northern* state being subjected to yet another instance of whites asserting their "supremacy."

I was also surprised by the confines of Saginaw's arrangement. At home in Indianapolis, although blacks mostly lived apart from whites, our neighborhoods were scattered throughout the city. And there were occasional areas, like the neighborhood I grew up in on the south side, where blacks and whites lived on the same street. There was also an upscale neighborhood on the north side, that we dubbed the Golden Ghetto, where Indianapolis's black elite—physicians, lawyers, entrepreneurs, preachers, and teachers—lived. The Indianapolis version of multiple racially separate neighborhoods was the only model I knew, so I expected to find a similar pattern elsewhere. I've since learned, of course, that each locale puts its own spin on keeping people separated by race insofar as possible. In Saginaw, all Negroes—seventeen percent of the 1960 population of nearly 100,000—no matter what their income or status, lived east of the river, and that included me. I was furious about how inconvenient this was, and let everybody know it.

I was employed at Douglas MacArthur High School on North Center Road in the unincorporated suburban community of Saginaw Township. (MacArthur merged with another high school and became Heritage High in the 1980s. The building I worked in is now the site of the White Pine Middle School.) The population in the township in 1960 was 15,619. Township residents were proud of their sleek new high school that opened three years before I arrived. If my memory is correct, the architecture of the school seemed more fitting for Florida or some other warmer climate. The school buildings were separate with walkways between them that were covered, but not enclosed. Most of the buildings, including the library, mocked the harsh Saginaw winters with a wall that was ceiling to floor glass.

I was the assistant librarian at the high school. And, in a pattern that has echoed throughout my life, beginning with my first job as a library page when I was fifteen, I was a member of the desegregation vanguard. MacArthur had an enrollment of 1,403 students, and except for perhaps a dozen Chicano students—children of farm workers who had settled in the area—a black physical education teacher, and me, everybody else in the school was white.

Sam Moore, the principal, reminded me of an absent-minded professor more than the stern authoritarian often associated with high school principals. He was about five feet nine inches, a little paunchy, with brown hair and eyeglasses. On my first day, he gave me a tour of the state-of-the-art facility. I met most of the other faculty including Harris Jackson, the black PE teacher who was hired the previous year. Harris was tall, handsome and charming, but, alas, married. MacArthur's white faculty and staff were either unconcerned about my skin color, or keeping their distaste to themselves; I had only one heated discussion with another faculty member while I was at MacArthur. It was with Rex O'Dell, who ran the audiovisual center adjacent to the library, but it was not about race. Rex was arguing that school district budget concerns could be resolved by *not* giving salary increases to female faculty. He said that since women did not have families to support, they *didn't need* to earn as much as men. Not only did I tell him how insulting that idea was to women, I also asked him what world he lived in where women did not have to provide for families. He stopped talking to me. Thank goodness.

The last stop on Sam's tour was the library. MacArthur had the largest and most elegant school library I've ever seen. It featured a circular fireplace and lounge area in a pit in the middle of the expansive room. The sunken space was carpeted, and the fireplace, undoubtedly the fulfillment of some architect's fantasy, was encircled by cushioned sofas. Nobody in their right mind would have lit a fire in a high school library, so the fireplace was merely ornamental. This centerpiece was flanked on the windowed side by the circulation desk, the card catalog, and tables and chairs for the students; and on the other side by rows of bookshelves not yet filled with books. During the two years I worked there, we acquired and processed over 3,000 new books.

Sam introduced me to the other library staff: Sally Hinkin, the library secretary, and Irene Galinas, the head librarian and my "supervisor." Sally was in her late thirties, petite and attractive with black hair. She was married with three children, the oldest of whom, Terry, was a popular student at MacArthur. Sally and I clicked and quickly became a team. She was smart, efficient, and gave me her unequivocal support. Sally made sure I had whatever I needed including not only supplies, but also background knowledge of the major players in the school and the Township, including inside information that clerical staff always have because they answer the phones and type the memos. (Or at least they did back then.)

A tall, slightly bent, white-haired woman, Irene was a proud white supremacist who wore her misery on her sleeve. She was the only person at MacArthur with whom I had an ongoing contentious relationship. Irene purposefully and gleefully did everything she could to humiliate or irritate me. Faculty avoided her insofar as possible, and the students ridiculed her, sometimes within her hearing. In addition to being crabby, she was no longer competent, if she ever had been. It shortly became clear that Sam was not happy with her, but hadn't figured out how to dump a tenured faculty member. Perhaps he thought having a black assistant would break Irene's fragile hold on propriety. I liked that Sam had not told Irene I was black. I could see that she was visibly shaken when we were introduced. At sixty-something and nearing retirement, Irene was dumbfounded that she'd have to share her work space with a Negro. As soon as Sam departed, she spewed her revulsion.

"And where did *you* get library training?" Her tone was doused in the certainty that no credible institution would ever have trained me as a librarian.

I didn't miss her tone or the implication, but I responded pleasantly, "At Indiana University. Where did you get yours?"

"Indiana University…? That's a good school." Irene's startled reaction indicated she was not expecting that response. Maybe she didn't know that IU admitted black folk. She paused to collect herself before spitting out, "Well, at least you didn't go to one of those awful little colored colleges."

I had heard all manner of racist insults, but this one caught me off guard; bigotry in the workplace was usually subtler. *Oh, this old woman is a real bitch. Well, it's good to know that up front so I can be on guard. If I'm not careful she'll run me out of here.*

That was merely Irene's opening gambit; from then on, she found as many opportunities as she could to say something detestable about all black people or about me personally. One of her most odious remarks occurred after I had been there for a few months. I was filing cards in the catalog and she stopped to speak to me. In a voice gilded with sarcasm she said, "I want to invite you to dinner, but I need to clean my house first. My house is so dirty I'll bet your mother's house is cleaner than mine."

Wow, this heifer has no limits, including playing the dozens.

She had to know I'd never eat anything prepared by her, so either she was knowingly playing the dozens, or thought she had finally come up with something that would make me go off on her. Considering how I felt about white supremacists who salved their fears and insecurities by abusing black people, I am astonished at how I dealt with Irene. No matter what she said, I never responded or told her what I thought of her. Nothing I said would have changed her attitude, and she was too addled and pathetic for me to reciprocate. I answered her insults by consistently doing an excellent job, and documenting my aborted efforts to work cooperatively with her.

Sally found Irene wearisome as well. We commiserated with each other, but also kept the library functioning despite Irene's ineptitude. Whenever Irene's venom spilled into what I perceived as a threat to my professional reputation, I immediately talked to the principal about it. Sam was always sympathetic and reassuring, so mostly I went about my work as if Irene weren't there. The students and faculty also ignored her, usually coming to me for assistance. When Irene observed that I was helping someone, she'd thrust herself between us and offer her own services. Each of us would quietly walk away then meet again to pick up where we left off before she interrupted.

I had a more serious problem than Irene. That fabulous-looking library did a number on me physically. I was logging a few miles a day walking the library's unyielding concrete floor with only a layer of linoleum tile between the cement and my high heels. The constant pounding jack-hammered my body into heavier and longer menstrual periods. I felt weak rather than sick, and some days I barely had the strength to get dressed and drive to work. To conserve what vitality I had, I found reasons to work in my office seated at my desk. I consulted a physician, but he had no more idea of what was happening to me than I did.

At the time, I was still living with my cousin's family and Odahlia suggested that I see their chiropractor. I didn't know what a chiropractor was, but I was willing to try anything. He realigned my body and strongly recommended that I give up my stylish heels for more sensible shoes. The shoes he proposed were flat, a neutral grayish beige color (is that called taupe?) with half-inch thick rubber soles that resembled tire tread more than anything else. They were not pretty, but as I returned to feeling like my usual self, they became quite fetching to me. I never left for work without them.

There wasn't much activity in Saginaw for single twenty-somethings, and a MacArthur English teacher, Lucy Smith and I bonded over that fact. We met when Lucy brought her classes to the library. We found lots to talk about because we were both in our first post-college jobs. Sometimes we had lunch together and on occasion went for TGIF (Thank God

It's Friday) drinks. One day we were discussing our separate but equally dismal housing situations when Lucy suggested that we could live in Fontaine Gardens by splitting the rent. Fontaine Gardens was an elegant and expensive new apartment complex about a mile from MacArthur. I had passed it many times, but gave it little thought because I'd already learned that I couldn't live in Saginaw Township, let alone in its swankiest new apartments.

"Lucy, I can't live there."

"If we share the cost, we can swing it."

"It's not the money. Negroes are not allowed to live out here."

"What do you mean, *not allowed*?"

"Lucy, have you ever seen any Negroes, other than Harris and me, anywhere in the township?"

"I don't know. I haven't looked. But so what? That doesn't mean Negroes *can't* live here!"

"Do you think that every Negro in Saginaw simply decided to live together on the east side? Have you ever heard of a ghetto? ...of housing discrimination?"

"Wait a minute. You're not telling me that *every Negro in Saginaw* lives in the same neighborhood? That doesn't even make sense! Do you live there?"

"What do you think? I'm a Negro."

Lucy was a naïve, inexperienced Catholic girl from a small town in Minnesota. Before she met me her only exposure to blacks consisted of watching civil rights activities on television. Like me, she had wanted a job away from home in search of something—new experiences, excitement.

"I don't believe this.... I can't believe this!" Lucy was becoming agitated. Like many whites, she believed racial discrimination was confined to the former Confederate States.

"Welcome to Negro life in America."

Chapter 2

Being Called to Struggle

*And still you are called to struggle, not because it
assures you victory but because it assures you an
honorable and sane life.*
~ Ta-Nehisi Coates

That weekend I picked Lucy up so she could see where
Saginaw's Negroes lived. Like my cousins, the Rance's,
many had comfortable homes, but I felt disrespected
because Negroes were not allowed to live outside a speci-
fied area. After driving Lucy around a bit, I took her to my
apartment. I had complained so much that my landlady
had put up drywall around the bathroom, but it had not
been painted, and the kitchen remained wall-less. Mrs.
Ferrell had accomplished her goal: she had a paying tenant. Obviously, it didn't matter that the apartment was not
presentable. After seeing my space, Lucy, who was renting
a room in someone's home, insisted, "Janet, we've *got* to
move to Fontaine Gardens."

"It won't be easy, Lucy, but I'm game if you are."

"I don't think we'll have a problem. It's 1964 and this is
not the South."

"I know *you* think that makes a difference, but it really
doesn't."

A few days later, Sam called me to his office.

"Lucy tells me that the two of you are planning to
move into Fontaine Gardens."

"We're going to try, but I don't believe they'll rent to me. Negroes aren't allowed to live on the west side."

"They won't refuse somebody who works for the township schools. And if they do, they'll have to answer to me!"

I was grateful for Sam's support, although not surprised. I had learned that over some objections from the school board, Sam had insisted that MacArthur's staff be desegregated. He also regularly checked with me to make sure things were going well. More important, he supported me when I had issues with Irene.

Lucy and I completed our applications for an apartment together and waited for a response. Although we made it clear we intended to share the apartment, her application was approved, but mine was rejected. When I asked why, the manager said, "We reserve the right to decide who can live in Fontaine Gardens."

I told Sam what happened and he called the manager demanding to know why I had been turned down. He told Sam I didn't pass the credit check. That was a bald-faced lie, and I told Sam so.

Sam went to Fontaine Gardens thinking he could personally persuade them to rent to me. He was practically foaming at the mouth when he told me about it. "The manager looked me in the face and said, 'We can't do it. If we rent to her, before you know it, they'll be swarming all over the place.' As if he was talking about roaches or something! They will *not* get away with this, Janet. We're gonna fight it."

I was somewhat amused at Sam's outrage; he had expected Fontaine Gardens to have some regard for an employee of the school system, but I knew that when it came to barring black faces, skin color outranked everything. I was happy however, that Sam was ready to go to the wall with me. I had not come to Saginaw to test racial barriers, but fighting racism was what we did in my family, so I was up for it.

Sam told me to contact Father Richard D'Onofrio, pastor of Saginaw's St. Paul's Episcopal Church and a member of the Saginaw Human Relations Commission (HRC). (I remember Father D'Onofrio telling me that he left the Catholic Church to follow his priestly calling as an Episcopalian because he wanted to marry and have a family.) After D'Onofrio put some pressure on Fontaine Gardens, the manager called me and said if I gave them a $150 deposit, they would *consider* my application. It was the "black tax" we are often required to pay. For black folk, things usually cost more than whites are asked to pay. Lucy had not been asked for a deposit with her application.

One hundred fifty dollars was more than a third of my monthly income. I had just finished college and relocated. I did not have $150, which is what Fontaine Gardens was counting on. I went to see Father D'Onofrio and told him what happened. Without hesitation, he picked up the telephone, called the manager at Fontaine Gardens and told him he'd get the $150 to him within ten minutes. The manager "hemmed and hawed and then said not to bother to send the money." Obviously, it was going to take more than informal pressure to put a stop to Fontaine Gardens' racist practices.

A lot of frustration had built up in Saginaw about housing discrimination, particularly the ban against black folks on the west side, but apparently, there had been no formal complaints. Because I was a young, educated woman who had moved to the area to work for the Saginaw Township school system, my situation was viewed as the ideal wedge to end the entrenched custom. The Negro librarian at MacArthur High School became a local cause célèbre.

D'Onofrio told me that the Michigan Civil Rights Commission (CRC) had enforcement powers and advised me to file a formal complaint with them, as I had done against Ludwick. The complaint against Fontaine Gardens, dated February 10, 1965, was more significant, he said, because it was an apartment complex and the owner had other properties. The CRC invited me to testify at their meeting in January 1965. I recall that during my testimony, being young and full of myself, I chastised local Negroes for not having eliminated housing discrimination before I got there. The following month, the housing issue and my case were the subjects of a "long, rancorous discussion" at a City Hall meeting of the Saginaw Human Relations Commission. On February 19, 1965, *The Saginaw News* reported on the meeting, and my name made the newspaper. I clipped the article and sent it to my mother. Forty years later, I found the yellowed clipping in her scrapbook. It was going to take a while to break the pattern of segregated housing in Saginaw. And it was not going to be easy.

Three days after that acrimonious city hall meeting, Malcolm X was assassinated.) My anger over his death turned to despair when I learned that he was killed, not by white racists, but by black men! How could they? No matter who was pulling their strings—Elijah Muhammad or the FBI—didn't they have any pride, any loyalty? I felt cheated and betrayed. Who would tell crackers the truth now? I first became aware of Malcolm X when I saw him on television in 1959 being interviewed by Mike Wallace. I had never heard or seen a black person being that forthright and honest with whites, on television no less! From that moment on, I wanted to know everything Malcolm X said or did.

It was many years later that I learned the FBI was secretly writing letters, tapping telephones, and generally creating enough chaos to turn Malcolm's rift with the Nation of Islam into an unbridgeable chasm. A year before Malcolm was killed, Elijah Muhammad had said, "This hypocrite is going to get blasted clear off the face of the earth," effectively ordering Malcolm's execution. To pay homage to Malcolm, I stopped having my hair straightened and started wearing an Afro. It was my way of announcing that I was a proud, militant, Malcolm X-type woman.

The following year other black folks picked up Malcolm's mantle and stopped being concerned about offending people who consistently offended us. California's Black Panther Party for Self-Defense organized in Oakland, and Stokely Carmichael, chairman of the Student Non-Violent Coordinating Committee (SNCC/Snick), issued a call for BLACK POWER. *That's what I'm talking about! YES!* And each new group was more assertive than the preceding ones.

This decade of ever more radical challenges to America's racism had begun in 1954 with the legal strategies of the NAACP (National Association for the Advancement of Colored People) in Brown *v.* the Board of Education; then Malcolm brought the separatist ideas of the Nation of Islam (founded in 1930) to national attention. In the meantime, freedom rides, boycotts and marches by CORE (Congress of Racial Equality) and SCLC (Southern Christian Leadership Conference) were taking place. These nonviolent efforts continued with the strategic sit-ins and systematic voter registration drives by SNCC. In a couple of years, I'd be cheering as the Black Panthers exercised their right to bear arms by striding into the California legislature carrying guns.

I wanted a more active social life than Saginaw had to offer for a young, single woman. Wurtsmith Air Force Base was located in nearby Oscoda and occasionally black guys from the base came to town. I briefly dated one of them, but otherwise my social and sexual life left much to be desired. I rarely met single men my age, and never at the house parties given by Odahlia and Rance's friends. All of them were married, and the wives were not particularly interested in having a young, unattached woman around. The best thing about those parties was that we had some good bid whist games.

Aside from the drama of trying to desegregate Fontaine Gardens, there wasn't much in Saginaw that appealed to me. I decided to enroll in a night class at the University of Michigan (UM) extension in Saginaw. I wasn't interested in working on another degree, but I had to do something about my insipid social life. Maybe I would meet some interesting men in a university setting. On the way to my first class meeting, I glimpsed a black man seated at the front of a classroom. Whoa! Was he a professor? I turned around and went back to the room I had just passed.

"What class is this?" I asked the fiftyish black man behind the desk.

"School Community Relations. It's a graduate course in education. Did you sign up for it?"

"Are you the teacher?" I hadn't had a black teacher since my *de jure* segregated elementary school; and I'd never had a black professor. I wanted to be sure this was for real.

"Yes, my name is Al Loving." He stood and held out his hand.

I shook his hand and said, "I want to be in your class." No way would I miss a chance to have a black prof. I immediately replaced the class I had signed up for with his.

Dr. Alvin Loving had been the first black teacher hired in Detroit's public high schools in 1935, and in 1956 the first black professor hired at the University of Michigan. Later he became a dean at Michigan, and on special leaves served in teaching and administrative posts in India and Nigeria.

His class reminded me of a sociology course I had dropped out of as an undergrad because I found it boring and ridiculous. But this time I enjoyed the social theoretic. Instead of being dismissive, as my sociology professor had been, Dr. Loving indulged my questions about the application of textbook theories to the experiences with which I was familiar. He may even have welcomed them since they were not likely to come from any other student; I was the only black in the class. One exchange I remember is that the textbook description of the middle-class sounded a lot like my family, but I had already learned that education and income put us firmly in the lower class. When I asked Dr. Loving about this he said that though my family's income was lower class, we had middle class *values*.

"As a result of the social and economic restrictions imposed on us, Negroes have created a class structure parallel to, but not matching that of whites."

I had no idea there was a class structure among Negroes. While growing up, I knew some black families were better educated and had more money than we did; but all of us attended segregated schools and none of us could work or eat downtown. During the summers, no matter where we lived, we could only swim in *one* city park pool. And Riverside, Indianapolis' amusement park, had a Whites Only sign in front. If there were class differences among blacks, they hardly seemed to matter.

While I was taking the course with Loving, I became friendly with another young woman I met in the library. We started hanging out together after we talked and discovered that we were both divorced and on the prowl. Sue was older than I, but still working on her bachelor's degree. She had dropped out of college to marry and have a family. We'd get together after class or on the weekends and complain about the dearth of single men in Saginaw. Sue had been married ten years when her husband left her and their three small children for his young secretary. That had been six years earlier, but Sue talked about him as if she had just learned of his betrayal. My own divorce was in its second year, but I was too enthused about new possibilities to have regrets or to think much about my ex. I presumed Sue was having difficulty letting go because her marriage had lasted longer than mine, and she had children. Unlike me, however, she received a divorce *settlement*. Without working she could maintain her family in their suburban home and take college classes! I'd never known a woman to do so well after a divorce. Not only that, but her family lived nearby and helped care for her children. Still, Sue seemed tormented. I was puzzled: why would an attractive white woman doing so well materially be distraught? Sue, on the other hand, couldn't believe how little I seemed affected by my "tragic" life—the death of a child and a recent divorce.

"Tragic? I don't think of my life as *tragic*! For the first time *ever*, I can do as I please and, believe me, that's not a tragedy."

There was no reason for me to hang around Saginaw, so when the school year ended in June, I went home for the summer. Some black folks in Indianapolis were horrified by my kinky hair. I got a few "right on's," but most, reflexively seeking social approval and acceptance, could not understand why I would expose my nappy head, especially in front of whites. Mama and my sister Rosie were particularly disgusted and didn't bite their tongues about it. Mama was so ashamed of my hair that she didn't even want me to go to church with her, something she usually insisted on. It seemed they had no idea that whites barely noticed us and cared little about what we did with our hair. A couple of whites at my job who did notice a difference in the way I looked merely observed, "You cut your hair." Indianapolis wasn't anywhere near ready for the changes the civil rights movement was stirring up.

I loved the coarse, kinky texture of my hair; it felt substantive. I had always dreaded those hot combs on my neck when the beautician was doing her damndest to get every little nap. I was glad to be done with the hair-straightening ritual. Although my mother and sister were mortified to be associated with me and my nappy hair, Daddy and my brothers either didn't care, or they were allowing the women to express the displeasure they felt. Mama begged me to get my hair straightened for Daddy's tribute banquet. I agreed so she wouldn't spend the evening in an agony of self-inflicted embarrassment. A year later, after Kwame Ture's (then known as Stokely Carmichael) powerful and persuasive orations about BLACK POWER, I gave up straightened hair for good.

I also went home that summer to help my sister. Rosie and Gordon's third anniversary present was the birth of Miguel Eugene, born June 28, a fourth grandson for my parents. My marriage "settlement"—living room and bedroom furniture—was stored in their two extra bedrooms,

Baby photo of Miguel

so I stayed at their house and slept comfortably in my own bed. Rosie didn't nurse Miguel, so when she came home from the hospital I got up at night, warmed his bottle, and fed him while she slept.

While taking care of my nephew, I was overwhelmed with memories of Paul, the son I had lost four years earlier. I had repressed my grief so thoroughly that I never consciously thought about the death of my three-month-old, but every time I looked at Miguel, I saw Paul. I had to get away. What I told myself, and anyone who asked, was that Rosie complained too much, not only about my hair, but also because she expected maid service as well as child care. I realize now that I was terrified of reliving that traumatic period of my life.

After the July 4th holiday, I asked Mama to take over with Rosie and Miguel and I fled to my little Saginaw apartment. That meant I had to come back to Indianapolis for Daddy's Testimonial Dinner on July 30, but a five-hour drive was nothing compared to the crushing reminders of my dead baby. I spent the remainder of the summer visiting my Lansing cousins and taking short trips with Nannie. She was my favorite cousin, probably because I knew her best. She and her husband Allen had lived across the street from us while I was growing up. I also spent a few

James C. Cummings presents Smith Cheatham with one of several plaques he received that night. (l.) Program cover for Testimonial Dinner

days with Gerry, a grad student I'd dated a bit at Indiana University (IU). His family had a summer place in Ludington, Michigan, and he drove over to Saginaw for a visit.

At the end of July, my father, Smith Henry Cheatham, was honored with a testimonial dinner for his "outstanding contributions to the progress of Indianapolis." The banquet was held at the Fall Creek Parkway YMCA, and the program read, "Through more than three decades of unselfish service to Indianapolis and its most cherished institutions Mr. Cheatham has contributed to the tenacity of his growing city."

My perpetually active father was the first black board member of the Indianapolis Redevelopment Commission, President/Founder of the Southeast Civic League, Board Member of the Fall Creek YMCA, Worshipful Master of Fidelity Lodge #55, F. & A.M., active member of the NAACP, Chairman of the Deacon Board and Superintendent of the

Sunday School at New Garfield Baptist Church. According to an article in *The Indianapolis Recorder*, about 500 tickets were sold for three dollars, regular admission, and five dollars for patrons. The entire family, including members of our extended family, was present for this grand occasion. Rosie, a talented organist played a solo as a part of the program. Daddy relished the attention, and I was pleased that he was receiving such well-deserved recognition.

In June 1965, the Michigan Civil Rights Commission ruled on my complaint against Fontaine Gardens and ordered them to (1) "accept the claimant's application..., (2) pursue an equal opportunity housing policy in all apartments..., and (3) instruct all managers in the implementation of such a policy." In the fall of 1965, nearly a year after my initial application to Fontaine Gardens had been rejected, Lucy and I moved in. The world didn't stop or even catch its breath. Nothing happened. If my presence in the previously all-white apartment complex disturbed anybody—aside from the recalcitrant management—we never heard anything about it. A few months earlier *The Saginaw News*, the city's only daily paper, published an editorial in the Sunday paper titled "Clergymen Face Test of Lowering Saginaw's 'Brotherhood Barriers.'" It referred to a recent "interfaith, interracial" meeting to "strike down the barriers to brotherhood so evident in the continuing practice of segregated housing." The editorial included the following statement, "The recently publicized case of a Negro school librarian...being refused housing in the West Side suburb affords a current example of the use to which [the Michigan Civil Rights Commission] machinery has been put."

The new apartment was all that I had wanted my first place to be. Although I was sharing the apartment with

Lucy, I had my own room and bathroom. We also had a spacious living room for entertaining guests, thick wall-to-wall carpeting, and a sleek modern kitchen. Because I was less than a mile from work I could sleep a little later in the mornings. My ex-husband was generous enough to load a borrowed truck with the furniture I had stored at my sister's house and bring it to Saginaw. That saved us from adding a furniture bill to the higher rent we were paying. As a result, Lucy and I had another couch in our living room to go with the sofa bed from my never-finished apartment at Mrs. Ferrell's.

The same month that I moved into my new place, on September 18, my cousin Diane Beanum married Jesse Merriweather and asked me to coordinate her wedding. Diane lived in Romulus, a two-hour drive away; her mother, Zeffie, was my dad's sister. Diane was younger by five years and had grown up in Michigan, but we knew each other well because our families had exchanged summer visits when we were children. I didn't know a thing about coordinating a wedding, but thought it might cause bad feelings in the family if I refused. Rosie had had a coordinator for her spectacular wedding, but Rosie, had directed everything herself, so I figured having a "coordinator" was more of a status symbol than anything else. I was a librarian, so I could have researched the duties of a wedding coordinator, but it didn't seem that complicated to me.

So, not wanting to refuse, and thinking it wasn't that important, I agreed to coordinate Diane's wedding and drove over to attend the rehearsal. As best as I can recall, the rehearsal did not go smoothly; there were too many people giving orders. Aunt Zeffie, an insistent figure in any setting, had specific ideas about how her only daughter's wedding should go. Diane, no wallflower herself, also knew what she wanted and I, the "coordinator," was consulted only when nobody had any idea what the protocol was for a specific instance. I usually didn't know either, but offered my opinion as if I did. On the day of the wedding, I was so nervous and insecure about my role that I arrived late to the church as the procession was about to begin. As flustered and confused as I was, I'm certain I contributed very little. My best hope is that I didn't totally botch Diane's special day. While I was writing this I asked her what she remembered of my involvement, but either she recalls less than I do, or she's too kind to talk about it. Tellingly, Diane has no pictures of me at the wedding although we agree I was present.

I earned an A in Loving's class and wanted to take another course from him. However, the Saginaw gig was an aberration; he usually taught on Michigan's main campus in Ann Arbor. He told me about a Saturday morning class I could take on campus. Hmmmm. If I took a Saturday class in Ann Arbor I could be out of Saginaw on the weekends! Driving the eighty-five miles to Ann Arbor after work on Fridays would be easy. I could spend the night with my relatives in nearby Romulus, and attend class on Saturday mornings. Who knew what might happen on Saturday night? This had definite possibilities! The Michigan campus would have tons of fascinating people, as well as lots of well-read black men. Whatever was going on there *had* to be livelier than Saginaw.

When I mentioned to Sue that I planned to take a Saturday class in Ann Arbor (A^2), she called a friend of hers who lived there. Sue thought Gloria would be a good contact since I didn't know anyone in A^2. Gloria graciously offered to have me stay with her when I came to town on the weekends. Perfect! I'd much rather be in Ann Arbor than driving over from Romulus.

Gloria greeted me warmly and I felt instantly comfortable. She was blond with some assistance, fortyish, also divorced, and had two teenaged children, whom I rarely saw. She was also active in the local CORE chapter, and I was thrilled when she invited me to join her at a CORE party the following weekend. Could I have asked for anything better? This was *exactly* what I was hoping for!

CORE was riding high in 1965. The civil rights group had been founded in 1942 by black and white students on the campus of the University of Chicago. They organized to desegregate public accommodations in Chicago, and after that successful campaign, they went national. Their biggest fame came in 1961 when they tested the legality of segregation on interstate bus travel in the South with their Freedom Rides. Because of CORE's origins, its members continued to be mostly black and white college students.

Gloria was white, but I knew there would be plenty of black folk at a CORE party. That meant I could easily meet some fine activist brother. I *knew* Ann Arbor would be an improvement over Saginaw. In those days, we dressed to look our best for parties—blue jeans had not become de rigueur for every occasion. When I packed for that second weekend in Ann Arbor, I included an outfit that always got lots of compliments: a chocolate-brown double-knit jacket and fitted skirt that I wore with a brightly-colored print blouse. I wanted to look so good that the brothers would feel like Monarch butterflies who'd spotted a zinnia.

Chapter 3

Needing a Change

*The need for change bulldozed a road down the
center of my mind.*

~ Maya Angelou

When we arrived at the party, every room on the first
floor of the spacious house was filled with people. *Yes!* The
majority were white, but just as I'd hoped there were also
lots of brothers. Gloria introduced me as we circulated.
Whenever I met a brother, I flirted demurely, but none of
them so much as made eye contact. Some of them looked
longingly at Gloria, but all I got was a cool acknowledg-
ment. Not one single brother expressed even the slightest
curiosity about me. What was going on here? Never had
I been in a social gathering in which I was completely
ignored by *every man in the room.* After about an hour of
this, I stepped back to scope out the situation.

An interracial party was a new experience for me; I
was accustomed to whites and blacks avoiding one another
socially. On Indiana University's campus, there was occasional and surreptitious dating across racial lines, but I'd
never been to a large mixed party like this one. I'd already
noticed that the crowd was mostly white, but in looking more closely, I saw that among the hundred or more
revelers there were a lot of black men, but only one other
black woman (Evelyn K. Moore, later co-founder and

president of the National Black Child Development Institute). And every brother there was either huddled with a white woman or eyeing one. I was definitely *not* what they were looking for. Interracial dating, furtive for so long, had erupted in the civil rights movement like Mt. Sinabung, the Sumatran volcano that was dormant for four hundred years. And the brothers were taking full advantage.

Well, fine. Two can play that game—I'll talk to the white guys.

I'd dated whites before, so this would not be unfamiliar territory. After my divorce, I dealt with feeling rejected, isolated and "homeless" by trying new experiences. I began to reinvent myself, or more accurately, to *be* myself. I determined to stop deferring to others' desires for what my life should be. It was not an easy process to change a lifetime habit, but I was completing college and about to become a self-sufficient woman. I plunged into a life that didn't resemble anything I'd done before. I was eager to explore, take risks, do whatever *I* wanted. I made new friends, often with people who didn't look like me or share my assumptions, beginning with the young women from Thailand, Taiwan, and Hong Kong with whom I shared a rooming house at Indiana University. Jessie Reiss, a Jew from New York and classmate at IU, became a dear friend. When she dated a rugby player, she introduced me to one of his teammates.

John was a tall blonde from England, and the first white man I went out with. Despite my apprehensions, it was not awkward. We had long, wide-ranging political and philosophical conversations much like the ones I'd had with Rickey Singh, a Guyanese man I'd previously met. I recall telling John during one exchange that growing up in Indianapolis I had only a limited number of hooks on which to hang information, and that I was now installing additional hooks. I also went out with Gerry, from suburban Chicago, who was in one of my classes, and later visited me in Saginaw. My dating was largely speculative; I wanted to meet a variety of people, but I was not interested in a serious relationship. Mama had trained me well not to trust men, saying they were mostly deceitful and unfaithful; my friends and I regularly referred to them as "doggish." My disappointing marriage simply reinforced my skepticism, so I was leery of men. Knowing the history of black women and white men, I was especially wary of their intentions. I craved masculine energy and the company of males, but I kept my heart to myself.

I looked around the CORE party for a promising target and saw a man who looked appealing. He was tall with dark hair and a beard, and standing alone in front of the fireplace. I walked over, struck up a conversation and soon learned that he *and his wife* were hosting the party. *So much for him.* I wandered into the dining room and saw another dark-haired, bearded guy standing in the doorway to the kitchen talking to a couple of people. (Not sure why I found dark hair and a beard alluring; perhaps I was being drawn to my fate.) He wasn't bad-looking, but short, not much taller than me. The subject of my attention had a white button bearing a black equal sign in the lapel of his jacket. After I pushed past him to go into the kitchen, I pointed to the button's familiar Urban League symbol and facetiously asked, "What does that mean?"

He turned to me and said, "It means equal rights for all."

"And does 'all' include people like me?"

"Of course. 'All' means everybody."

Arthur Alan Saxe

I looked him in the eye and said, "I've seen very little evidence of that."

He grinned, held out his hand, and said, "Hi. I'm Art Saxe. What's your name?"

Art was also visiting A² for the weekend, having driven down from Mt. Pleasant to attend the party and visit friends and fellow CORE members. I learned that he was from Brooklyn, New York, and a dissertation away from a PhD in anthropology at the University of Michigan. He had recently moved to Mt. Pleasant, a small college town fifty-three miles west of Saginaw, to teach sociology and anthropology at Central Michigan University (CMU). CMU was founded in 1892, as the Central Michigan Normal School and Business Institute, with classes in teaching, business and stenography. In 1966, 7800 students were enrolled, half of them in teacher training.

This was the first time I'd met a professor socially, but he wasn't pompous as I might have expected.

Art and I talked for a while then he disappeared. I didn't see him again until the party was winding down and those who remained were gathering to watch him perform. Accompanying himself first on guitar then on banjo, Art sang traditional folk songs from various cultures including a couple of blues numbers. I was impressed that this white guy knew my people's music. I hadn't thought white folks were interested in black music unless they were making money from it. When Art finished playing he walked directly over to me.

"Can I take you home?"

We rode to Gloria's house in his cream-colored Volvo (a car I'd never heard of), and sat for a while chatting. He asked if he could see me again, so we exchanged phone numbers. Art was polite, keeping his hands to himself, giving me only a quick peck on the cheek after he walked me to the door and said goodnight. That was a point in his favor; I despised guys who tried to grope you the minute you were alone. I was more than a little intrigued by him— a single professor from New York City, *and* active in the Civil Rights Movement! This could be interesting. But I didn't expect him to call, and I wasn't about to call him!

Art called on Monday and asked me to join him for an event in Mt. Pleasant the following Saturday. That meant after my class in A^2, I'd drive back to Saginaw. I was not, however, also going to drive to Mt. Pleasant; I told Art to pick me up at home. I didn't want him to think I was so entranced I'd come to him! Art drove the fifty-something miles to Saginaw, picked me up and we went back to Mt. Pleasant for the event. Then he drove me back home. And that's the way our courtship went. If Art wanted to see me, he had to come to Saginaw.

Not only did Art play black music on his guitar and banjo, but he had an impressive collection of blues albums at his apartment. Lightnin' Hopkins, Sonny Terry, and Brownie McGhee were among the blues albums he had amassed. He also owned the Library of Congress recordings of Muddy Waters and Huddie "Leadbelly" Ledbetter. His library included books like *The Souls of Black Folk* by W.E.B. Du Bois and James Baldwin's *Nobody Knows My Name,* and he had *read* them. I didn't know many black folk with whom I could discuss these and similar books. The more I learned about this man, the more appealing he became. And I was flattered when he told me he had come to the CORE party with another woman but took her home so he could return and talk to me.

"You know you're a stereotype." I teased Art. "You're a Jewish scholar from New York City whose parents have retired to Miami."

Not only that, but upon his arrival in America, Art's father (or was it his grandfather?) had changed the family name from Schechtman to Saxe. And, of course, the family had money. Art insisted that his family was not wealthy; and they didn't have old-money-from-the-slave-trade wealth, but compared to my family, *they had money.*

After a couple of months Art grew weary of driving to Saginaw every weekend.

"Why don't we move in together and get a place half-way between here and Mt. Pleasant?"

"Are you kidding? I'm not going to *live* with you!" *Those days are over, buddy!*

"But I'm not ready to get married."

"Who said anything about getting married? If you're tired of driving here every weekend, come over every *other* weekend." I was aghast that he thought I would *shack up* with him! My family and friends would be horrified if I allowed a *white* man to use me like that.

In my mind, I put the developing relationship with Art on hold because I needed to focus on my new responsibilities. I have never liked getting up early in the morning. Usually I struggle, and often fail, to show up for anything at what I consider the ungodly hour of 8 a.m. This inclination to sleep in was put to a test when I was promoted to head librarian my second year at MacArthur High. That meant I'd have to open the library every morning. Irene Galinas had been transferred to the district's central office where she would work with materials instead of people. So long as Irene was responsible for opening the library, my arrival somewhere between 8:00 and 8:30 was not particularly significant, although she enjoyed upbraiding me about it. I was always there before school opened for the students at nine. Sally, the library secretary who always had my back, pulled me aside after we found out about the promotion.

"Janet, you're going to be in charge now so you've got to be here on time. We don't want them to regret getting rid of Irene. Okay?"

"You're right, Sally. I'll be here." Living closer to work and knowing that I would not be greeted by Irene each morning helped me make good on that promise.

No way had I expected to be promoted to head librarian, and I was shocked that Irene was kicked upstairs. She must have been hysterical when she found out the "colored girl" she had regularly insulted was replacing her.

Lucy, my roommate, was named as my assistant. At the time, I assumed she preferred working in the library to teaching. However, as I write this I wonder: Was Lucy the only person who was willing to work under black supervision? (When you've encountered personal and institutional racism every day of your life, it is nearly impossible not to suspect every situation of having that stain.) Sally, Lucy, and I worked well together, and with Irene gone, the students relaxed and used their grand library more often.

As part of the research for this book, I examined pages from the MacArthur High School Yearbook for 1965-66. I had not previously seen this yearbook, so imagine my surprise when I saw the page depicting the library staff. A large picture of Sally was featured in the center of the page. Smaller pictures of Lucy and me assisting students were placed left of Sally's photo. The description referred to us as "the three librarians." I suppose this misrepresentation was meant to obscure the actuality that a black woman was running the library with two white women reporting to her. In addition, I was reminded that Sam Moore had been replaced as principal in my second year at MacArthur. I have no idea what happened with Sam, but my first thought was that he was removed because of his push to desegregate MacArthur. Also, his support of my efforts to remove the ban against blacks residing on the west side of Saginaw probably didn't go down well either.

Art didn't like my suggestion that he visit me every *other* weekend; he wanted us to spend more time together, not less. Not long after I rejected his suggestion that we move in together, he asked me to marry him. I thought he was crazy; we'd only known each other a couple of months, but instead of emphatically turning him down, I said, "Let me think about it."

The next time we saw each other Art said, "Janet, we need to go shopping for clothes to get married in."

"Clothes to get married in? What are you talking about? We're not getting married. I told you I'd think about it!"

"Seriously...? I thought you were just being coy." Art was genuinely surprised.

"Coy!? We barely know each other."

"We know we want to be together, and you won't move in with me, so we have to get married. I've applied for the license, and made an appointment for us to get blood tests. And a guy in my department is planning a reception for us at his place afterward."

Woohooo! This man reeeeally wants me! He won't take no for an answer. Not that I ever said, "No."

This white professor wants to *marry* me! I knew this was a risky, if not absolutely foolish, proposition. I had not intended to marry again any time soon, if ever, but marrying someone I hardly knew was insane! However, the more I thought about it, I decided this could be an intriguing adventure!

We went shopping and Art bought an expensive dress and shoes for me, and new jacket, slacks, shirt and tie for himself. Then he showed up one day with the marriage license. I had no idea he could get a license without my being present. Obviously, I was wrong. When he started talking about the reception in Mt. Pleasant, it dawned on me that I might be the only black person there. I hurriedly invited my cousin Odahlia and her husband. I also asked a new friend, whom I'll call "Marian," to attend. Marian had agreed to go out with us when Art's former roommate—the tall, brilliant, black and fine Jamaican, Richard Thelwell—came for a visit. I was sufficiently uncertain and embarrassed about the hastiness of the marriage that I did not invite anyone else, specifically not family and friends from home.

In the days prior to our marriage, Art called his parents to let them know he was getting married again; like me, he had been married once before. I heard what he said and afterward he shared his mother's comments with me.

"Ma, I'm getting married. Her name is Janet and she's a Negro."

Art and I had discussed this. I thought it would be better to let people discover what I looked like when we met. But Art was eager for everybody to know he was marrying a black woman; it "proved" that he was indeed a political radical.

"A Negro!" He reported his mom said this with alarm. "A Schvartze? But they're not our people!"

"Well, Ma, you know the Yemenite Jews are black."

"Oh! Is she Jewish?" Art said his mother sounded somewhat relieved at that possibility.

He admitted I was not Jewish. I suppose that comment was meant to assure her that if there were black Jews somewhere in the world, people of my hue were not irredeemable. Of course, I doubt that Yemeni Jews think of themselves as black.

Art then wanted to know how my parents might react. "What about your parents? Will they have a problem with me being a Jew?"

"No, not at all. My mother just wants me to be married. So far as your religion is concerned, she'll be happy to know that you have one."

Despite my cavalier assessment of how my mother would respond, I hadn't told my family about the upcoming marriage. How would I explain that less than two years after shaming them by getting a divorce, I was marrying again—to a man I barely knew who was also *white*? I couldn't think of a way to justify it, or any compelling counter argument if they tried to talk me out of it. It would be easier to tell them after the fact.

So, once again I was getting married with trenchant misgivings. But I had my reasons. For starters, Saginaw had not delivered the kind of excitement I was hoping for when I left home. More important, however, I was dazzled by Art's intellect, his world travels, and his fluency in all manner of topics unfamiliar to me. Not insignificantly, I am also a contrarian. In the race-conscious culture of the U.S. I knew that the sheer novelty of my marriage to Art would shock some folk and irritate others.

Before Art and I left on our honeymoon, I told my family I'd gotten married and gave them my new address. Mama was furious. "I can't believe you'd be so foolish!" She was not concerned that I had married again, but rather that I had married a *Jew!* Before long I learned that Mama wasn't the only one; other blacks were also offended. Some accused me of joining the enemy, and others were puzzled as to how I could allow a *white* man to touch me after the hell they'd put us through. A small group of black folks, however, applauded me for "landing" not only a white professor, but a *Jew!* Everybody knew that Jews have money, so I had hit the jackpot so far as they were concerned.

It was 1965, and nearly all marriages—99.6 percent—were between people of the same "race." Rarer still were marriages where the woman was black and the man white. The custom was that white men didn't need to marry a woman to do as they pleased with her, whether she was black, white, married, or single. A woman's only immunity from being fair game was the protection of a powerful white male. Any black man who objected to the exploitation or abuse of a woman could be brutalized or killed with impunity. W.E.B. Du Bois, the scholar, historian, and activist who was a founder of the NAACP, put it this way. "To the ordinary American or Englishman, the race question at bottom is simply a matter of ownership of women; white men want the right to use all women, colored and white, and they resent the intrusion of colored men in this domain."

White men's (the wealthy and powerful ones particularly, but not exclusively) use of women of African descent began with the Transatlantic Slave Trade, and became an established American tradition passed from one generation to the next. Their freedom to have any woman they wanted, whether the woman was willing or not, is the reason there's such a medley of skin colors among black people. This abuse was institutionalized most famously in antebellum New Orleans with a system called *plaçage*. The plaçage began with a formal ball where wealthy men—French, Spanish, or Creole (free people of color)—selected a concubine. These men were often married and holding other Africans as slaves. The women on display had one-quarter, one-eighth or less African ancestry and were correspondingly labelled quadroon or octoroon. They were young, chaste, highly prized, and chaperoned by their mothers, who were often in plaçage themselves. The mothers negotiated with the wealthy men to obtain the best "deal" that would provide for and protect their daughters, and any children of the union. The negotiations were to be completed before the man could claim the young woman as his own. These women, of course, no matter how infinitesimal their African heritage, had no recourse, legal or otherwise, if the man reneged on his promises.

After slavery was abolished, powerful white men continued to peremptorily have sex with black women, often women who were their domestic servants. One of the major reasons black folk worked so hard to educate their daughters, was to preclude their having to accept positions in domestic service where they were at extreme risk of being raped. A high-profile case in point was Essie Mae Washington-Williams' revelation in 2003 that she was the daughter of the late segregationist U.S. Senator Strom Thurmond of South Carolina. Her teenage mother was a servant in the Thurmond household when Strom, in effect, raped and impregnated her.

No "respectable" white man, however, ever *married* the black women with whom he had sex. And even when a white man wished to marry, he was barred by laws forbidding, not only marriage, but openly cohabiting with a black woman. There were rare occasions where white men pretended to be black so they could live openly with the black woman they loved. On the other hand, if a white woman was discovered having a clandestine relationship with a black man, her terror of being ostracized, and possibly brutalized, would likely make her claim "rape." That accusation was tantamount to a death sentence for the black man, who would be lynched without receiving a trial or even being questioned.

Whatever the nature of the interracial relationship, it was not to be sanctified or legalized by marriage. In fact, most states had at some point considered such marriages to be as verboten as same-sex marriages were until 2015. In 1965 when Art and I married, sixteen states had laws that made marriages between blacks and whites a criminal offense. A few months before we married, my home state of Indiana legalized interracial marriages by repealing a law passed in 1818 that banned not only marriage between blacks and whites, but also sexual intercourse. Michigan had repealed their ban on marriage between the races in 1883 so we could be legally married there.

Two years later, in 1967, mixed marriages became legal throughout the country. The U. S. Supreme Court in Loving *v.* Virginia declared that laws banning such marriages were a violation of the equal protection and due process clauses of the fourteenth amendment to the Constitution. Interestingly, the case was brought by Mildred and Richard Loving, a black woman and a white man. Three percent of married couples were mixed in 1967. Since that ruling made such marriages legal, the number has risen to seventeen percent of newly married couples.

In 1883, the Supreme Court had ruled that interracial marriages were *not* legal, a ruling, ironically, also based on the fourteenth amendment. That case, Pace *v.* Alabama, was a marriage between a black man and a white woman.

With this history and social climate, I knew my marriage to Art would be an anomaly and that we might travel to places where our marriage was against the law. In addition to welcoming that challenge, I was curious about experiences about which I knew little—the academic world, Jews, and white people. It would be a complete change; a totally different life from anything I'd been involved in before!

On a cold Saturday afternoon, December 18, 1965, Arthur Alan Saxe and I were married in Isabella County Michigan. He was thirty and I was twenty-eight, both Taureans with May birthdays. The ceremony took place at the simple rural home of a Justice of the Peace whose yard was thick with mud. Boards were laid between the car and front porch so we could get inside without muddying our shoes. Witnessing the brief ritual were Art's younger sister, Sharon, in from New York; Dan and Miriam Levenson, friends of his who drove up from Ann Arbor; my new friend Marian from Saginaw; and my roommate Lucy, maid of honor. After the license was signed and a couple of pictures taken, we went directly to the reception, at the

Wedding party: (l-r) Marian, Dan, Miriam, Art, me, Lucy, and Sharon

home of one of Art's colleagues.

I don't remember much about the reception. There were a few wedding gifts and some refreshments, but I don't remember who was there besides our witnesses and my Saginaw cousins. I had not thought about a honeymoon, considering the dispatch with which we got married, but as a wedding gift, Art's friends Lew and Sally Binford sent us airline tickets to Santa Barbara, California. We were on winter break, so made the trip right away. It was my second trip by air and first visit to California. Another friend of Art's gave us an expensive hi-fi set with detached speakers. Nobody I knew could have spent that kind of money on wedding gifts. As I anticipated, life with Art was going to be different.

Art and Lew Binford had become friends while they were both grad students in the Anthropology Department at the University of Michigan. Art often said that Lew was the smartest person he'd ever met. Lew, who was thirty-five when we visited them, had earned his PhD from UM four years earlier in 1961. He was tall, robust, blustery, and renowned in the field as the leader of the "new archeology." Sally, also a brilliant anthropologist/archeologist was lean and dark-haired, six years older than Lew. She and Lew sometimes collaborated in their research and writing. They were both teaching at the University of California in Santa Barbara. The university had a nepotism rule prohibiting two people from the same family from having full-time jobs within the Cal system. Consequently, befitting the era, Lew had the full-time job and Sally was hired as a part-time lecturer.

My mother saved a postcard I wrote her from Santa Barbara on Christmas Eve. I gushed, "It's so beautiful here! I wish we could live out here. …Our house is on a mountain side with a view of the Pacific on one side and the mountains on the other."

Sally and Lew's large home was decorated with fascinating artifacts from their world travels. It was perched on the mountain in a way that though there were other residences nearby, the outdoor pool was not visible to them. I went skinny dipping for my first and only time. In December, no less! It was wonderful to feel the water caressing every part of my body. Unrestricted! No swim suit with its customary and always ill-fitting padded chest interfering with my movements while the bottom of the suit cut into my thighs. Art also introduced me to unfettered sleeping, a practice I've continued. No more of the frothy, so-called sexy, nightgowns that had always twisted uncomfortably around my body. I find it more sensible not to have restraints while you're sleeping, and particularly when you're making love; and Art was a skilled and inventive lover.

The visit and honeymoon were marvelous—more intoxicating in every way than my first honeymoon. We had sumptuous meals accompanied by wine and passionate, sometimes combative conversations about anthropology and current social and political issues. I liked Sally and admired her marrying a younger man. She was obviously a free-spirit, warm, hospitable, and an artful and excellent cook. (Evidence of Sally's singular spirit is that she decided at age fifty that she did not want to live so long that she became a burden to others. Before her 70th birthday, she put her affairs in order and committed suicide.)

These many years later I still recall two of her dishes: a roasted goose stuffed with sauerkraut that had been marinated in dry red wine, and a dense, rich cheesecake made from scratch using three different cheeses. I never attempted the cheesecake, but I duplicated her goose a few times.

That week in Santa Barbara was unforgettable and hard to leave, especially knowing that we were returning to icy snowbound Michigan. I liked California so much I eventually went there to live, but that's getting way ahead of my story.

Chapter 4

The Sound of the Genuine

There is something in every one of you that waits and listens for the sound of the genuine in yourself. It is the only true guide you will ever have. And, if you cannot hear it, you will, all of your life, spend your days on the ends of strings that somebody else pulls.

~ Howard Thurman

The summer following our marriage, Art and I drove to Indianapolis for the weekend so he and my family could meet. Despite Mama's active disapproval of the marriage, I knew she would be a gracious host, no matter how she felt about her guests. When I saw that she had called in reinforcements, however; I knew just how uncomfortable she was. Art and I were greeted on arrival by the whole family including my siblings and their spouses, plus my cousin Norma and her white boyfriend. I imagine Mama invited Norma because she thought Art would be more at ease if there were another white person present. This considerate gesture was nullified by her refusal throughout the weekend to speak directly to Art. As we left to return home, Daddy followed us out to the car. My six foot tall muscular dad bent over on the driver's side to look directly into Art's eyes.

"You're alright with me. I don't care nothin' 'bout color so long as Janet is happy and you treat her right." I suppose that was his way of not only apologizing for Mama without embarrassing her, but also letting Art know that he expected him to treat me "right."

Some years later Mama accused me of having set a terrible precedent because younger members of our extended family, in addition to Norma, have dated and/or married whites. If my marriage to Art opened family members to other possibilities, as it did for me, good. I doubt, however, that my decision had anything to do with their choices.

My mother was an intelligent, well-read woman, but there were complex systemic obstacles blocking her from fulfilling her career dreams. Instead, like many women of her generation, she turned her talents to volunteer work and supervising her home and children. Mama stayed in regular contact with James, Reggie, Rosie (my siblings) and me; we were "her" children. Mama was more attentive to our lives than Daddy was, probably because he had other interests in addition to his grown children. As we got older, Mama's dominion over us grew increasingly tenuous, but that simply made her more persistent. She often talked one or more of us into putting pressure on the sibling who wasn't doing whatever she thought they should. This created friction among us, which meant there were times when we were so upset with each other that the only person we were speaking to was Mama.

Among my many attempts to make Mama happy, I remember writing a long letter to James chastising him about his relationship with his wife, Dodie. *He was in Vietnam at the time!* Even if I had actually observed him mistreating his wife, which I had not, *it was none of my business*. But Mama had insisted that I write James about

My siblings and I with our spouses: (l-r) Dolores "Dodie" in front of my older brother, James; Art, me; Reggie, Bonita ("Bonnie"); and Gordon Mickey behind my sister, Rosie.

something she and Dodie had discussed. And I did as she asked. I can't believe I had the nerve. Ugh! As if I owned some wisdom about relationships, marital or otherwise.

I suppose I hoped that by occasionally doing something Mama wanted, it would compensate for the many times I had disappointed her. Despite her entreaties to my siblings, they all told me they refused to join her crusade against my marriage. Instead, they told her she was being unreasonable. They also reminded her of Jews who had been supporters of equal rights for black people, like Arthur and Joel Spingarn who helped start the NAACP. It took a while, but Mama eventually accepted Art, probably convinced by James' explanation that Jesus was a Jew. Before she came around, though, she gave me the blues.

Mama's calls and letters focused relentlessly on the perils of being married to a Jew. Since the people in my parents' social life—church, civic activities, friends, relatives—were all black, Mama's essential interaction with Jews, or any whites, was cleaning and doing laundry for them. Mama resented this work, being convinced she was meant for more intellectual pursuits; and she was, but those opportunities had not been readily available to her. Her opinion of whites and Jews was shaped by a lifetime of encounters with racial discrimination and her well-founded perception that whites regarded her primarily as a work horse. During one of her tirades against Art she told me emphatically, "Be very careful because Jews will work you to death."

"Ma, I don't work for Art; he's my husband." To her, he was a white oppressor who had the additional stigma of being a Jew. I so dreaded reading her letters full of dire warnings that I asked her to stop writing if she had nothing else to talk about.

She responded by calling me, "I'm doing this for your own good because you don't know what you're doing. You're such a foolish child! Always have been. You don't know these Jews like I do."

"Alright, Ma. That's enough! Just leave me alone. Do not write. Do not call. I can't listen to this anymore." And I hung up the phone.

I don't know that my mother ever thought of me as anything other than "a foolish child." If she did, she didn't share it with me. Her default position was pointing out my many shortcomings: I was too big, my hair was too short and nappy. I was the first in my entire extended family to graduate from college, but she was disappointed that I didn't finish in four years. I distressed her further by getting divorced and moving away from my hometown. Now I had married a Jew! I interpreted her disapproval of nearly everything I did as evidence she didn't love me. And if your own mother doesn't find you worthy of love,

My family of origin. Reggie standing in back, and me sitting in front. On the couch, my sister Rosie, Daddy, Mama and older brother, James.

who will? I was self-conscious because I saw myself as my mother described me, and I was defensive in anticipation of rejection. Fortunately, my father's pride in each of his children, helped me feel that I had some merit. His approval, the fact that I did well in school, the praise of employers, and my relentless curiosity, kept me from being overwhelmed by self-doubt.

I was forty-two years old the one time Mama praised me, and remember it vividly because it was so out of character. I had just purchased a home in Boston where I worked for a book publisher; something I had aspired to since childhood. Mama and I were talking on the phone and, sounding amazed, she said, "You've really done well for yourself." I think she was puzzled that the dismal consequences she had predicted for me because I didn't "have a husband" and wouldn't "get somewhere and stay put," had not materialized. I was thrilled that she approved of something I'd done.

A short while after I asked Mama not to write or call, I was surprised to receive a thoughtful letter from Daddy. After each of us moved away from home, Mama became the conduit to Daddy. She wrote the letters and made the calls to their children. Daddy only talked on the phone when one of us asked to speak to him. Otherwise, she told him what she wanted him to know and told us what she wanted us to hear. That's the way it was in our family, and we never questioned it. Not wanting to be cut off from me, Daddy continued to write and call regularly throughout the hiatus with Mama, which lasted more than a year. I have no doubt Mama encouraged him, but they were *his thoughts*, not messages from Mama. He wrote about his community involvement, news of my siblings and people I knew, and what various family members were up to.

Meanwhile, Art had the last laugh on me. After we married, we lived in Mt. Pleasant, so *I* was the one driving to Saginaw—*every day* to go to work, often on icy roads. I definitely had the better apartment, but I had a roommate, so we moved into Art's place on the first floor of an old frame house at 410 East Wisconsin. The landlady, Sadie Higgins, lived on the upper floor, but we used the same washer and dryer. Each of us had access to the laundry room through different doors that could be locked behind us when we finished. Art had not thought it necessary to inform Sadie he'd married a black woman. When she unlocked her door to the laundry room and saw me doing laundry, she smiled and closed the door, assuming Art had hired a maid. A black woman *working* in her house was the natural order of things. After a while, Sadie learned I was Art's wife, *living* in her house.

She was horrified.

Of course, Sadie was right to approach Art because he was her tenant; but I've always been intrigued by the cowardice of white supremacists. The ones who deny their racism, in particular, seldom have the courage to confront the people they want to banish. And even those who flaunt their bigotry usually ambush their targets, or gather in mobs to carry out their heinous acts. Sadie told Art he had to move immediately. Then she locked the door to the laundry room so we could no longer wash our clothes.

Art was outraged. "She can't do this!" He thought he was rather savvy about racial prejudice because he was active in CORE, had been president of the U of M NAACP, and no doubt had been discriminated against as a Jew. However, during our marriage he was repeatedly aghast at the kind of treatment America reserves for black folk.

"I'm calling the police! She can't force me to move because I married a Negro!"

"Where have you been? The police don't care. People are always telling Negroes where we can and cannot live. The only difference here is that it happened *after* I moved in."

"She is *not* getting away with this!"

"I don't care what happens to her. She's not the first racist I've ever seen, but I don't want to live under the same roof with one." Who knew what she might do; after all, she had access to all of our things. I wanted out of there, probably more than she wanted us gone.

Art was not having it. He raised hell at Central Michigan University (CMU) until they sent an official letter to Sadie warning her she would be removed from their list of approved housing if she didn't back off. The threat to her pocketbook was magical. Access to the laundry room was restored immediately and we didn't hear another word about being evicted. Sadie was no longer smiling and friendly, but who cared? I was still determined to get out of her house. Sadie's racism only made worse the bad matter of *paying* to be in a dumpy old house with outdated wiring.

I do have some pleasant memories of my six months in Mt. Pleasant. On one occasion Art invited some colleagues and their wives, including his department chair, to dinner. Art was nervous about entertaining them. We both cleaned the apartment and prepared the meal for the event. I cooked a goose à la Sally Binford and it was a huge hit. If it was a wife's job to make her husband look good, I had triumphed. Art beamed with pride at every compliment. We were a social success. After our guests left, we both cleaned up. I was surprised that Art helped out because I was accustomed to men who didn't do anything in the kitchen except look for food. I found it endearing that without my asking, Art shared all the household duties—cooking, cleaning, doing laundry. I had built up a ton of resentment in my previous marriage because my then-husband believed women were supposed to serve, pick up, and clean up after their husbands. My mother had also taught me that such things were "women's work. It didn't make sense to apply that relic from the past to a lifestyle in which we both got up and went to work every morning.

One of Art's students was James Turner, a brilliant young black man from New York City majoring in sociology. He and his wife Janice came for dinner a couple of times and we talked about the burgeoning civil rights movement. A few years later in 1969, James established the

Africana Studies and Research Center at Cornell University. After I began teaching black literature, I ran into him a few times at TransAfrica gatherings, and also at African Heritage Studies Association conferences.

Another pleasure during my marriage to Art was that for the first time in my life I did not have to pinch pennies. When we married our combined annual salaries were over $12,000, at a time when the median family income in the U.S. was $6,900. I truly enjoyed being able to buy and do whatever I wanted without agonizing over prices. We could travel by air as often as we chose, and when I shopped for groceries, I bought expensive steaks like the ones served when I worked as a maid. I also got any other treat I desired—the creamed herring Art introduced me to, and the dry wines we had with dinner. Our liquor cabinet was always amply stocked, partially because Art enjoyed several cocktails every evening, but also because, in a distinct departure from my upbringing, serving liquor was an integral part of entertaining guests. And we entertained often. Art took pride in his ability to make pizza from scratch, including spinning and tossing the dough, and he had pizza-making equipment—a rolling pin, large flat pans and circular pizza knife. When friends came over for a casual evening, Art would make large thin-crust pizzas with lots of toppings.

Despite these amusements, I did not want to stay in Mt. Pleasant; it was smaller and duller than Saginaw. I especially wanted out of Sadie's house, not to mention how sick I was of driving to Saginaw every day. I leaned on Art about moving to Ann Arbor, encouraging him to finish up his PhD and get a professorship in a livelier place, or maybe even another country. Either I was persuasive, or he was also ready to leave.

Regina Cheatham

Grandpa Cheatham
holding Gregory (l.)
and Miguel

That June I resigned from MacArthur, and Art left
CMU. In A^2 we sublet Apartment #3 at 808 Tappan for
the summer and looked for permanent housing. While
we lived in that apartment, Daddy came to visit without
Mama. When my parents visited Mama's relatives in Lansing, Daddy drove alone to Ann Arbor to see us. That was
undoubtedly the first time Daddy had traveled to visit one
of their children without Mama along. We had a great time
with him because he was a joyful, gregarious person.

That summer of 1966 my parents also celebrated the
birth of their first granddaughter. Regina Cheatham was
born August 15 to my younger brother Reggie and his wife
Bonita. Three months earlier Mama and Daddy had welcomed their fifth grandson, Gregory Ramon Cheatham,
born May 3 to James and his wife, Dodie.

Art and I found a well-kept two story frame house on Spring Street in Ann Arbor and signed a year's lease. It had a living room, dining room, and large kitchen on the first floor, and two bedrooms and a bathroom upstairs. Neither Art nor I had ever had that much living space, and we loved it! The things from both our prior apartments were sufficient to furnish our home. And because we had room, our house became a gathering place for friends, meetings, and parties. When Floyd Mc Kissick, the successor to James Farmer as national director of CORE, came to town we were honored to have him spend the night in our spare bedroom.

I had rarely spent time with intellectuals. Books were important in my family, but we didn't have long, in-depth discussions about what we read. On occasion while I was a student at Indiana University, we would debate ideas, but among my first-generation-college friends, our energy was primarily focused on getting enough to eat and meeting the requirements for that all-important degree.

Being with folk who regularly questioned conventional wisdom, talked about why things happened, and compared positions from the books they were reading, was invigorating. In this circle nearly everyone had a degree, and several were engaged in advanced graduate study. We hung out with all kinds of accomplished people, including archeologists, artists, community organizers, medical students, and physicists. I was an eager participant in examining all manner of topics—the escalation of the war in Vietnam, the civil rights movement, organizing protests, the merits of religion, cultural mores, economics, politics, including the recent election of Edward Brooke to the U.S. Senate, the first black person since Reconstruction. And, though the discussions were intense and often contentious, nobody ever seemed angry. I couldn't get enough of it.

In addition to the visionaries and activists I was familiar with—W.E.B. DuBois, Mary McLeod Bethune, Paul
Robeson, Thurgood Marshall—I was introduced to others,
like Saul Alinsky and Michael Harrington.

Art was a Marxist, a term I had heard, but knew little
about. He was so passionate about it, that I listened carefully to his arguments. He and his friends talked about dia-
lectical materialism, the theoretical framework of Marxism. I understood the concept of class struggle, as well as
their insistence that communism was a better economic
system because capitalism exploited workers and enriched
only the owners of capital. I had never thought of exploitation in other than racial terms, but Art was determined
that I see oppression as primarily economic.

"Think about your father, Janet. Supposedly, in the
capitalist system if you work hard, you'll get ahead. Your
dad has worked hard all of his life. If hard work was all that
it took, he should be rich by now!"

"Hmmmm. That makes sense." And it sort of did,
but the explanation did not completely satisfy me. I still
struggle to parse what economic system is most efficacious
for large, complex, and now global, social organizations.
Not that *I* should be able to figure it out when most econo-
mists can't. Soviet communism broke down, and capitalism collapses regularly and nearly wipes out everyone
except the small percentage with the vast majority of the
money. Although they may lose net worth and be fearful of
losing more, the haves usually *remain wealthy*. Meanwhile
the financial gap continues to widen between the haves
and the have-nots. And it doesn't appear to be much different in countries that are allegedly communist. According
to *Newsweek*, "91% of 3,220 Chinese citizens worth 100
million yuan ($14.6 million) or more, are the children of

high-level Communist Party officials." Apparently, no matter what the economic system, the money flows to those in power and remains there. Neither communism nor capitalism is immune to greed and corruption.

As I listened and thought about new ideas, I yearned to follow my own guidance about what I believed and how I wanted to live. As far back as I could remember, I had chafed at the demands of "authorities"— my parents, teachers, employers, and husbands. I was developing the courage to pull my own strings.

I began with cosmetic changes. First, I stopped straightening my hair, and now I decided to have my ears pierced, something I had wanted to do for years, but my mother had forbidden it. She pointed out a relative who'd wound up with a keloid scar on each of her pierced ears and promised the same thing would happen to me. I'd seen only one person with keloids and dozens of people with pierced ears who had no scars at all, so I decided to go for it. A med student friend of ours pierced my ears. A few years later, I had another hole added to each ear, making me a full-fledged heathen so far as Mama was concerned.

I was adjusting to going wherever and doing whatever we wanted without hesitation or second-guessing! Art was accustomed to moving with confidence in any environment, a new experience for me. We might be the object of stares and double takes, but nobody *ever* said anything rude to us, at least not within our hearing. The long looks seemed unfriendly to me, but Art welcomed our presence startling people. We casually went into elegant restaurants, hotels, and shops which I would have been hesitant to enter alone. Some maitre d's and salesclerks were obviously surprised, but always polite. Late one night we were driving on a back road somewhere in Michigan, and Art needed to use a restroom. He stopped at the first open gas station, and my immediate thought was he shouldn't get out of the car in such an isolated place. Then I remembered, "He's white; nothing will happen."

And, oh happy day, I discovered that apparently body size, as well as beauty, is in the eye of the beholder. One Saturday morning some close friends stopped by for breakfast. After we finished eating we were chatting around the table when I overheard Art say, "Janet can eat anything and never gain a pound."

I was jolted to hear that being said about *me*. I had spent my young life agonizing about being overweight. My mother, my brothers, and my previous husband had regularly taunted me about being too big. For the first time in my life there was nobody needling me about being fat. Plus, I was so exhilarated by new experiences and concepts that I hadn't thought about my weight, so maybe I had lost a few pounds. After overhearing Art, who was lamenting that he had gained weight since we married, I joyfully realized he didn't think of me as fat!

Much of the dialogue in our house centered on anthropology. My interest was stirred by the talk about various ethnic groups Art and his colleagues were studying in different parts of the world. I'm not sure I'd ever heard the word "anthropology" before I met Art, but I was fascinated by the similarities of people in various places, no matter how simple or complex their social organizations. Art's dissertation topic was "The Social Dimensions of Mortuary Practices." I asked what that was about.

He said, "I'm examining the ways different cultures dispose of their dead. Usually, the higher an individual's social status, the more people are involved in the end-of-life ceremonies."

"Like when a famous person dies, lots of people line up to pay their respects?"

"Exactly! And it seems to be true, no matter what kind of society it is."

Art gave me an article to read titled, "Body Ritual among the Nacirema" (American spelled backward) by Horace Miner, one of his professors at Michigan. I was intrigued by it because it presented familiar things from a different angle than the one I took for granted. Miner puzzled over the American penchant to equate the value and status of a house with the number of bathrooms it had. I liked the article enough that I decided to enroll in some anthropology courses.

I had been admitted to U of M for my prior course work as "not a candidate for a degree." I was taking those classes primarily to expand my social life. After the arduous struggle to earn my bachelor's degree, I was too relieved and emotionally drained to submit to the grind of pursuing a degree again. However, I did enjoy taking classes for the fun of learning.

Art said it didn't make sense to take classes without being formally admitted and insisted that I apply to the Rackham School of Graduate Studies. Although I'd received two A's in the U of M courses I'd taken previously, my GPA as an undergraduate was a C. I wasn't surprised when there was no response to my application. I expected to be denied, but decided to call and learn my status before I enrolled in classes.

"No, Janet. You don't want to call them." He knew about my undergraduate grades and why I was hesitant. "Go *visit* the graduate office, they won't turn you down to your face."

I thought indeed they *would* turn me down to my face, but figured I had nothing to lose by following Art's suggestion. At the graduate office, I told the receptionist why I was there. She went to a file cabinet and found my folder which included a 5" x 8"-sized form. She read the form then placed a check mark in the box beside "admitted," and handed me a carbon copy. I was stunned. A receptionist had just admitted me to the University of Michigan graduate school. I had merely inquired, and it was done!

I felt like I had just learned a white-people secret. Without Art's insistence, I wouldn't have considered making a personal visit to the office. Not that I am reticent, but I had been thoroughly indoctrinated not to assert myself—it wasn't ladylike, and more important, drawing the attention of whites might remind them of how much they loathed you. I had learned it was best to remain quietly amiable around the people who could, on an impulse, make your life extremely difficult. Art, of course, had no such thoughts. That's when I learned I had been accepting rejection *before* encountering it. On the other hand, the receptionist was black. Maybe she was just doing a sistah a solid.

The first anthropology course I enrolled in was a two-hour undergraduate class on North American Indians. I also took courses in Primitive Religion and Primitive Economics at Michigan. Studying anthropology and talking about the classes with Art helped me see racial strife in the U.S. from another perspective. I learned that the conditions of black people in this country are much like those of oppressed people in other places. African Americans are not the only aggrieved people, and skin color not the only reason people are persecuted. I was discovering that human behavior is the same around the world. Groups just have different social practices and rationales for their mores. We are all alike. The more I learn, the more that understanding has been reinforced.

I also began to question what I'd been taught about God. I found out there were people in the world who had thrived for centuries without any concept of the Judeo-Christian religion. That meant what I'd been taught about the universality and indispensability of Jesus-Jehovah wasn't true for everyone. People outside "the western world" believed their gods to be as powerful as we did ours; and all gods apparently do the same thing: abate our fears of misfortune, illness, and death. The anthropology texts were written with a Euro-American bias, so their approach to the religions of less complex societies often implied these cultures were operating at a level inferior to that of monotheists. They referred to these gods as *fetishes* (an inanimate object that has spiritual power) or dismissed the people as unsophisticated *animists* (a belief that everything in nature and the universe itself has a soul). After reading contemporary spiritual seekers like Deepak Chopra, Shakti Gawain, and Gary Zukav, I've come to think that these "primitive" beliefs are more reflective of universal spiritual wisdom than many contemporary Christian credos. Moreover, I see no difference between fetishes and the Catholic church's images of saints. The hierarchical religious organizations and imposing physical structures of Christianity, Judaism, Islam, have influenced some to think of them as more important than belief systems that don't have these intimidating material symbols.

Art, a non-practicing Jew, said, "The Unitarians have the best idea because they pray to whomever it may concern." This was typical of Art's disdain for religion.

He also had some amusing thoughts about Christians. "Christians see God as a double-entry bookkeeper, sitting on high debiting sins and crediting good works. If they finish their lives with more credits than debits, the accountant lets them into heaven. If not, they burn in hell forever."

I had to laugh at that because it was definitely a reasonable interpretation of what I'd been taught.

The tenuous hold of the Baptist absolutism I'd learned while growing up was loosening. As a young child, I'd secretly questioned the idea that a loving God would gladly and vengefully make me burn in hell for all eternity if I continued to "sin." It was impossible not to offend God regularly, so I was burdened with guilt about all kinds of trivial things. I also had the blasphemous idea that Jesus was not God; I believed he was human like the rest of us, which is what made him special. I knew my parents would be upset and frightened for my very soul if I mentioned any of this, but it didn't stop me from having the thoughts. What a relief to meet people who openly debated religious doctrine; their skepticism was as refreshing as it was liberating.

Chapter 5

Distorting Language

By stretching language we'll distort it sufficiently to wrap ourselves in it and hide.

~ Jean Genet in *The Blacks*

That year in Ann Arbor was pivotal to my cerebral life. I could not have articulated it, but *this* was the excitement I was hoping for when I left home. I craved an environment of seeking, scrutinizing people with whom to share my curiosity about everything. Mama always said that I asked more questions than all three of my siblings put together. The life Art and I created, revealed another layer of myself to me. I believe he discovered some things he didn't know about himself as well.

Despite the level of intellectual exchange, racial insensitivity was still on display. Many of those who are regarded as white are inclined to perceive people of African descent as less than themselves, no matter how "progressive" they are. We were hosting a party in our home when a female guest standing next to me, reached over and swirled her fingers in my hair. It was not the first time I'd been imposed on in that way. I immediately responded by swirling my fingers in her bouffant hairdo. She recoiled in horror and sternly said, "Don't do that, you'll mess up my hair."

"You just messed up my hair!"

"I just wanted to see what it felt like."

"Then *ask* me if it's okay to touch my hair!"

I have no idea why so many women of European descent are eager to know how the hair of black people feels. (In my experience, it is only they who must touch my hair—no men, or people of Indigenous, Asian, Latin, or Middle Eastern descent have ever taken that liberty.) These women, who are *always* offended when I respond by digging my fingers into their hair, never think about how I feel when a stranger sticks her hand in my hair. Satisfying their curiosity is all that matters. This absence of concern for me occurred on one particularly stressful evening. I was waiting in a hospital emergency room and focused on comforting my critically ill brother who was lying on a gurney. Suddenly, I felt a hand in my hair. I jerked my head around and saw the back of a woman, in what appeared to be a nurse's uniform, rapidly walking away. I was furious! That bitch! How dare she?! I wanted to snatch a knot in her tail, and would have gone after her had I not been attending my brother. It's probably best that I couldn't.

Such racial blunders as these, however, had far less impact on me than Art's decision to stop performing sexually. Within the first couple of months of our move to Ann Arbor, Art apparently lost interest in me, or at least in having sex with me. It didn't happen all at once; his activity declined gradually. At first, he responded when I worked to arouse him, but after a while, nothing I did, and I mean *nothing*, could get him to an erection. It reached a point that if I was affectionate in bed, he became irritated and asked me to leave him alone. I left him alone.

I was especially vulnerable to rejection. My previous husband had spent nights away from our bed early in our marriage, and when I decided to leave him and go back home, my mother turned me away. Art's refusal to touch me aggravated my doubts about whether I was worthy of being loved. I couldn't figure out why he had lost interest in me. Otherwise nothing changed; Art was as attentive and affectionate as he had always been. Except when we were in bed. To further complicate the matter, when we were with friends, most of whom were people he had known for years, he groped me and made randy comments. This public fondling was no doubt designed to make people think we were tearing it up at home. Humiliating me further, Art "playfully" squeezed the nipples of the women in the circle of five interracial couples we spent a lot of time with. I was astounded the first time I saw him do it.

I pulled him aside. "Why would you do that? What the hell are you thinking?!"

"I'm just playing around. It doesn't mean anything."

"Well, stop 'playing around'! You can't go around putting your hands on other women's breasts!"

But he did it again the next time we all got together. I was appalled and embarrassed by his asinine behavior. The next time I saw him pull on a woman's breast, I called him out.

"Art, how would you feel if I went around grabbing men's dicks?" Everyone present seemed to gasp in unison.

Defiant and angry Art fired back, "It's not the same thing! Touching a man's penis is a sexual act. I'm just playing around."

"Are you crazy? Touching a woman's breast *is a sexual act*! What if some man walked up and grabbed my breast?"

One woman, then another spoke up, making it clear they did not welcome Art's "playfulness." He acted surprised, and tried to laugh it off, saying he didn't mean anything by it. The nipple pinching stopped, but that didn't have any impact on our sex life; it remained nonexistent.

I was surprised that the men in our little group hadn't intervened the minute Art touched their wives' breasts. Was it because in our circle of interracial couples, except for Art and me, all the men were black and the women white? Did the black men think this was how white folks carried on? It wasn't happenstance that we mixed couples hung out together; we weren't welcome everywhere. In 1966 relations between blacks and whites were fragile at best because the country was involved in an explosive civil rights movement making headlines nearly every day. A year earlier an uprising had taken place in Los Angeles' Watts neighborhood. It was shortly followed by several urban rebellions around the country. The atmosphere in nearby Detroit was building toward one that took place the following year, and lasted for five days.

The rising tensions in the country did not bypass Ann Arbor. Perhaps the four black men in our social clique thought the consequences would be grim if they confronted or assaulted a white man, no matter how he insulted their wives. I presumed Art took such liberties because his impotence had damaged his sexual esteem. To make himself feel better, his default response was to demean women and black folks; the traditional privilege of America's white males. I cannot imagine an all-black group where any man would be brazen enough to openly fondle the breasts of another man's wife/girlfriend *in his presence!* And if it happened, she and/or the man would put a stop to it immediately. Clearly, Art was contemptuous of women, but would he have dared touch their breasts if they had been with white men? What I know for sure is that Art never pinched a nipple when we were in a gathering where I was the only black person present. The nipple-pinching insolence may also have been Art acting out the turmoil and insecurity he felt around educated black men; each of the men in our little interracial group had advanced degrees.

Ah, racism; the progenitor of myriad offspring.

In this volatile racial environment, the U.S. House of Representatives voted to unseat Adam Clayton Powell Jr. in January 1967.

We black folks were outraged! Because of Powell's fierce and public opposition to racism, he was a revered figure to my family and most black folk. In 1964, shortly before I graduated, I had the privilege of hearing him speak when he came to Indiana University's campus. Powell was everything I had expected from having read about him and seen him on television—confident, engaging, well-informed and quick-witted.

In 1945, Powell was the first African American elected from New York to the U.S. House of Representatives. Some members of Congress disliked him intensely because he insisted upon being treated with the same respect as everyone else in the House. He ignored their racist traditions and took full advantage of the congressional restaurants, press stations, and recreational facilities. Powell became chair of the House Committee on Education and Labor In 1961, and in that pivotal position, he led an unprecedented number of legislative reforms. He spearheaded an increase in the minimum wage, educational resources for the deaf, student loan funding, job training and the regulation of work-hours. His demonstrated legislative prowess on top of his personal pride, made Powell unbearable to his fellow legislators, and they voted to refuse him his duly-elected seat. Their action was declared unconstitutional by the U.S. Supreme Court.

More significant even than Powell being restored to his seat, was that in October 1967, President Johnson appointed Thurgood Marshall as an Associate Justice of the U.S. Supreme Court.

Although we African Americans had long thought we should be represented in every branch of our government, Marshall's appointment was a surprise. We didn't expect the first black justice to be an uncompromising advocate for civil rights like Marshall. But then Johnson had surprised me before. I was not happy that a southerner became president when Kennedy was killed. I had lots of qualms about southern whites. My skepticism was based on history, and on what I was seeing on television as African Americans resisted legalized racial segregation. Lyndon B. Johnson, however, turned out to be the former Confederate states worst nightmare. In speaking to congress about passing the Civil Rights Act of 1964, Johnson said, "We have talked long enough in this country about equal rights. We have talked for one hundred years or more. It is time now to write the next chapter, and to write it in the books of law." After tremendous pressure generated by the revulsion over the brutality of police to marchers on Selma's Edmund Pettus Bridge, Johnson pushed through passage of the Voting Rights Act of 1965. That legislation overturned the barriers most southern states had erected to prevent black people from voting.

I suspected that Art, like Powell's fellow members of Congress, and many white Americans, was uncomfortable with capable, well-educated, confident black men. Aside from his former roommate, Richard Thelwell, who was back home in Jamaica when we were in A², Art's closest black male friends were a police officer and a taxi driver. Alex and Walter did not have college degrees; Art met them when they worked together in CORE. We discussed racism, politics, and the civil rights movement, but they were not academics. Richard, who had master's degrees in both public health and business, was apparently the only educated black man with whom Art was comfortable. His reaction after we returned home from a party gave me more reason to believe he was intimidated by brainy black men.

As soon as we walked in the house, Art exploded, "The only thing he has on me is that he's black."

The party was given by someone outside our usual circle. I still remember the name of the man I met that night, Ken Simmons. We had a long, engrossing conversation. He was intelligent, charming, and knowledgeable. Our intellectual exchange crackled with a soul connection. I talked to him most of the evening, secretly lamenting that I couldn't go home with him. He may also have been married; we didn't exchange personal details. I was oblivious to everything and everyone else at the party except Ken, and Art noticed. We were silent on the ride home— he was agitated; I was pensive.

Art followed me into the kitchen where I went to get some water. I knew what he was referring to, but feigned ignorance. "What are you talking about?"

"That guy you were talking to all night. The only reason you were so carried away was because he's black. He's no smarter than I am!" Art, who probably had more to drink than he should have, was loud and angry.

I remained nonchalant, "We were just having a conversation. I don't know what you're talking about."

Art picked up a jar of jelly and hurled it against the

kitchen wall. The glass splattered and grape jelly stuck to the wall next to the kitchen stove.

That frightened me. I'd never seen him violent. "What's wrong with you? Have you lost your mind?"

He responded derisively, "Clean up that mess."

I screamed at him. "You must be crazy! You made the mess. You clean it up!"

"I wouldn't have made it if it hadn't been for you." This was the first of several tantrums Art had, and he always insisted that I was responsible for his blow-ups.

"You *have* lost your mind if you think I'm going to clean that shit up."

I stomped off to bed fuming. Art made a big show of sleeping in the guest room for a few nights. He may as well have slept there every night for all the use he was in bed. We barely spoke for several days, and the jelly remained on the wall until we had the house cleaned when we moved out. We never talked about that night again.

I didn't think of it at the time, but I've since pondered whether Art's insecurity around educated black men contributed to his sexual impotence. On the other hand, he may have just been ambivalent about his sexual orientation.

Art responded quite differently after another party. Archie Singh, a grad student from India and a friend of Art's, threw a big party to celebrate completing his doctoral degree. Some familiar friends were there, but also people from several countries and diverse academic disciplines that I rarely saw or had never met. There was lots of good music and dancing. I was wearing a black and white sun dress with a full skirt and feeling flirtatious, probably because I was horny. I danced with a lot of men,

74

rarely sitting. For a long time, until it was eclipsed by other momentous occasions, I remembered this as one of the most fun parties I'd ever attended. Art didn't dance, but he seemed to have a good time eating, talking, and watching me. When we got home he was still elated, chatting about what a great party it was. He got an unassisted erection that night. He was all over me the way he had been before we moved to A^2. I surmised that he was savoring the idea that he may not have danced with the belle of the ball, but he got to take her home. I believe that was the last time we had sex.

Because neither of us wanted children, I was taking the birth control pill, which in those early days of the pill's development, had higher doses of the synthetic hormones than they do currently. I had disturbing side effects, the most disquieting of which was a dramatic change in mood just before my period. I'd become deeply depressed, lack energy, and not want to do anything. These feelings escalated gradually until in my tenth month on the pill, I was feeling suicidal. We weren't having sex anyway, so I stopped taking the pills and in about three months, I was back to my usual self. I never took them again. Before I stopped taking them, I'd put them out where Art couldn't miss seeing them as a reminder, I hoped, that we should be having sex. He completely ignored my ploy.

When I tried to talk to Art about our sex life, he wouldn't discuss it, except to tell me, "Sex isn't important to intellectuals. It preoccupies uneducated people because they have nothing else to think about."

I considered that rationale for a while, in my mind substituting "whites" for "intellectuals" and "black folks" for "uneducated people." I had spent my life to that point uncritically accepting the notion that people of European descent had power and wealth because they knew more about everything than we black folks did. Perhaps we did spend too much time and energy on sexual concerns. Maybe that was why white people were more successful than we were. We had always laughed about white people being cold, emotionless creatures more concerned about money and power than the joys of life. Maybe it was true! Fortunately, since then I've learned about the systemic racism integral to American institutions, both public and private, that operates to limit opportunities for African Americans' success. It is also apparent to me, of course, that despite these built-in privileges, not all white people are powerful and wealthy, and not all black people are poor and weak.

I distracted myself from my sexless marriage by focusing on the other things I was busy with—the classes I was taking and my new job. I was the librarian, and one of three female staff members, at the Whitmore Lake Boys Training School (BTS). Whitmore Lake, an unincorporated community ten miles from Ann Arbor, is the site of a detention facility for juveniles. The stated purpose of the school is "to rehabilitate delinquent youth, ages 12 to 20, who have been adjudicated for felony offenses and placed at the Training School by court order." It was either difficult to find educators willing to work with incarcerated youth, or the salaries in the Detroit area were higher than in Saginaw. In any case, I was making thirty percent more per year than I earned at MacArthur.

There were three hundred boys under age eighteen being detained at the facility, some in a maximum-security building. All the boys who weren't on restriction for some infraction were brought to the library for a period every day. I was astonished to see such young boys locked away from their families, and heart-broken that seventy-five to eighty percent of them were black—a pattern that is entrenched in the penal system throughout the country. The boys' accounts of how they got there introduced me to a world of despair and flawed justice that I had known little about. Sometimes I retreated to my office in tears after listening to one of their stories. Boys were sent to BTS for everything from murder to school truancy.

I talked to them not only about the books, but also asked about their lives. I considered one young man's tale a definite miscarriage of justice. He appeared to be about nine years old.

"Why were you sent out here?"

"They said I molested a girl."

"Did you molest her?"

"She was my girlfriend, but they said I molested her because she was eight."

"How old are you?"

"Fifteen."

Good lord! He was so small and childish looking, I'm sure no girl his age would have taken him seriously. I learned that when he was eight years old he had seen a man kill his mother. That trauma no doubt arrested his physical growth and maturation; no wonder he seemed lost and bewildered. He needed help, not punishment. I wanted to hug him, but that wasn't allowed.

Another inmate, a fourteen-year-old white boy, was locked up for being truant from school. He had gotten a job to help feed the family because his mother was sick and he had no idea where his father was. He was anxious and depressed because he didn't know how his family would eat without him at home to provide for them. His despondency and worry were heavy on my heart.

My co-workers told me I was too softhearted. They said I shouldn't be moved by what the boys told me; that none of it was probably true anyway. I knew that some of the street savvy drug dealers, and one nineteen-year-old pimp who had bought his way into BTS to avoid adult prison, were jiving me. However, many of those young men were telling the truth, and the fact that I couldn't do anything to help them just tore me up. One day when a high-yella boy appeared in the library, I got another reminder of racism's progeny. His appearance initially startled me, but I quickly understood why. He was the first light-skinned black inmate I'd seen at BTS.

The school was participating in Daniel Fader's reading program, Hooked on Books, and as librarian I worked with that program. Dr. Fader, then an assistant professor of English at the University of Michigan, was the author of *Hooked on Books*, published by the U of M Press in 1964. His program replaced traditional classroom texts and workbooks with paperback books, newspapers, and magazines. The objective was to provide reading materials the boys liked, material that related to their lives, and to use that material to develop their reading and writing skills. Dr. Fader, who insisted I call him Dan, believed that we had to begin teaching the boys where they were before we could lead them to where they could be.

Instead of being lined with bookshelves, the BTS library displayed the paperback books on multiple spinning wire racks, like the ones then found in drugstores. One of my tasks as librarian was to periodically drive the fifty or so miles to Detroit to the wholesale distribution company that donated materials to the school. Dan took me the first time, showed me around, and introduced me to the staff. Afterward I went alone and selected new books to fill the library book racks. Aside from detective mysteries and adventure stories, I discovered that the boys preferred real-life books to fiction. Occasionally one of the young men became interested in a book of essays like *The Fire Next Time* by James Baldwin, but they usually read stories of people's lives like *The Autobiography of Malcolm X* with Alex Haley and *Manchild in the Promised Land* by Claude Brown.

Ossie Davis, the late actor, playwright, and activist, visited BTS while I was working there. I think he was performing in Detroit and somebody, probably Dan, wanted him to see what we were doing with Hooked on Books. I remember him as having a powerful, sensual bearing.

Since using the library was a privilege withheld from those detained for serious violent offenses, or who were considered incorrigible, I had only a couple of encounters that were appreciably different from my interactions with the students at MacArthur High. The most surprising one happened while I was working in my office after the library was closed for the day and the students were back in their residences. I suppose I felt a presence. I looked up and about thirty feet away saw a sixteen-year-old blonde white boy on the other side of the glass of my enclosed office. I recognized him because he regularly came to the library, but we'd never talked. He was quiet, and seemingly quite shy. When I looked up, I was shocked to see that his fly was open with his penis jutting out. That startled me and I let out a yelp that sent him scurrying away. When I went to the school office to report what had happened, I learned that the student was somehow roaming around the school and had also exposed himself to a female teacher. I have no idea what happened when they found him; I never saw him in the library again.

The young black pimp with the well-paid lawyer talked my ear off when he was in the library. He scoffed at people like me who worked a regular job, saying they couldn't possibly make the kind of money he made. He was continuing the family business, having been trained for his career by his dad. When I pointed out that the women working for him weren't making that kind of money, he sneered, "They're lucky to have me. I take better care of them than their mamas did." He told me how smooth he was and bragged about how much his girls loved him, saying he could easily spot a potential hooker. He also believed he could talk any woman into working for him, including me. I laughed out loud at that, reminding him that he was locked up! As he promised, his time at BTS was short, no more than a couple of months, proving yet again that money talks and bullshit walks.

During that year in Ann Arbor, I also spent a lot of time rehearsing for a play. A friend told me that a local production of Jean Genet's *The Blacks* had been unable to find anyone to play the part of the Queen. I tried out and got the part, probably by default. *The Blacks* is an existential allegory set in Europe and Africa. Many people consider the ritualistic play, subtitled, *A Clown Show*, to be inflammatory. In it, the murder of a white woman by a black man is re-enacted by black actors for the entertainment of an audience of white establishment figures—the Queen, a high-court judge, a bishop—played by black actors wearing white masks. *The Blacks*, which became the longest-running off-Broadway play of the 1960s, has been described as "not commercial, but confrontational, and it doesn't dramatize racial stereotypes so much as boil them in a pot, dance around them, and dish them up for dinner."

I was fascinated by this difficult play and its abstract, confusing language, and I enjoyed playing a character. We rehearsed several nights a week as opening night approached. It was grueling, especially with a full-time job and keeping up with my classes at U of M. There were nights when I truly didn't feel like rehearsing. And Art, who couldn't bear to be alone, grumbled that I was never at home. Finally, he demanded that I withdraw from the play, and I did. They found someone to take over my role, but after betraying my cast mates, I was too embarrassed to go see the play.

That capitulation was uncharacteristic, but less than two years into the marriage, I couldn't admit I had failed again. If deferring to Art's wishes would make our marriage work, I was willing to try it.

Chapter 6

Trying for Wings

Well married, a person has wings; poorly married,
shackles.

~ Henry Ward Beecher

"I am not going ten thousand miles from here to help murder and kill and burn poor people simply to help continue the domination of white slave masters over the darker people."

Teach, brother! Muhammad Ali, a member of the Nation of Islam/Black Muslims, made this public declaration on April 28, 1967 after he refused to be inducted into the U.S. Army.

YES! Like Malcolm X and Stokely Carmichael (later known as Kwame Ture), Ali was doing the unthinkable, speaking his truth to powerful whites. I was gratified to see him take that position, and to watch him refuse to back down when the retributions were launched. Ali was right; black people needed to be fighting for freedom *here*, not somewhere else. He inspired us all.

As Cassius Clay, he had been celebrated for winning a boxing gold medal at the 1960 Olympic Games. Carmichael's admiration for Ali began, he said, when Ali announced his name change during a press conference just after he won the heavyweight title from Sonny Liston. Ali told the media, "I don't have to be what *you* want me to be." Carmichael said that's when Ali crossed "that media-imposed line of 'responsible' black protest." Most white journalists seemed insulted by Muhammad Ali's public declaration that he would be himself, and not make any effort to be acceptable to white supremacists. This simple statement was considered incendiary because white supremacists believe they should control the pronouncements and behavior of black folks.

The ire over his new name, however, was mild compared to the rabid denunciation of his refusal to be drafted into the army. Ali knew there would be reprisals for the stand he was taking. The savage fury unleashed by the news media was swift and meant to destroy him and his career. Except for those of us already opposed to the war, it seemed the entire country hated Ali for his refusal to fight people who, as he said, "had never called [him] a nigger." The New York Boxing Commission immediately took away Ali's boxing license and his heavyweight title, and the World Boxing Association shortly followed suit. In a federal court, he was convicted by an all-white jury of draft evasion and sentenced to five years in prison.

Second only to my admiration of Ali's fearlessness, was my glee over the group of men who stepped forward to support Ali. In June 1967, a group of prominent black athletes, and Carl Stokes—later that year elected mayor of Cleveland, Ohio—held a press conference in Cleveland. References to this event usually focus on Jim Brown, Kareem Abdul-Jabbar, and Bill Russell. I am still so grateful for the courage of all the participants that below I name all the men present that day. Much like Colin Kaepernick and his twenty-first century supporters, these active athletes jeopardized their livelihoods to protest the historic and systemic oppression of African Americans.

Publicly supporting Ali were Lew Alcindor, a UCLA basketball player, who changed his name to Abdul-Jabbar; Gayle Sayers, Chicago Bears; Walter Beach and Sid Williams of the Cleveland Browns; Jim Brown, an actor recently retired from the Browns; Willie Davis, Green Bay Packers; Curtis McClinton, Kansas City Chiefs; Bobby Mitchell, Jim Shorter and John Wooten from the Washington Red Hawks, all National Football League (NFL) teams, and Bill Russell, who had recently been named player-coach for the National Basketball Association's (NBA) Boston Celtics.

Before he stood with Ali, Walter Beach had been labeled a troublemaker by the NFL's Boston (now New England) Patriots. The Patriots had accepted segregated accommodations for the team in New Orleans, where they were scheduled to play a preseason game. The white members of the Patriots were set to stay in a luxury hotel, but the black players were assigned to rooms in the homes of black families. Beach organized the black players to protest their separate lodgings, and the Patriots cut him from the team in 1963.

Martin Luther King Jr., who also opposed the Vietnam War, praised Ali for his "courage and sacrifice." Other black leaders—among them Roy Wilkins of the NAACP, Whitney Young of the Urban League, and Edward Brooke, U.S. Senator from Massachusetts—thought it was a mistake to link the civil rights movement to the movement against the war, and publicly censured black opposition to the war. I had no respect for "leaders" who were more interested in the blessing of people who oppressed African Americans, than in what was best for us.

The wielders of power fear few things more than aggrieved whites coalescing with African Americans and
other marginalized groups. They have historically, persis-
tently, and successfully fanned the flame of white supremacy to forestall such cooperation. The FBI did what it always
does and added Ali to the distinguished company of black
people they had under constant surveillance. At various
times this group has included, Marcus Garvey, Elijah Muhammad, Pearl Primus, Eslanda and Paul Robeson, W.E.B.
Du Bois, Thurgood Marshall (who became a U.S. Supreme
Court justice), Ella Baker, and Malcolm X. At the same
time as Ali, Carmichael and King were being watched and
tracked as well.

Ali never served his five-year sentence, remaining free
on bail while his case was appealed all the way to the U.S.
Supreme Court, which overturned the conviction in June
1971, two years before the Vietnam War ended. We were
jubilant that Ali had been vindicated, but by then he had
been suspended from boxing for three and a half years and
lost millions of dollars in potential income.

Art regularly ridiculed the Nation of Islam's dogma,
but he unequivocally admired Ali's boldness. We both
knew that defying white supremacy and the United States
government was a daunting prospect for anyone, but it was
an especially terrifying action for a black man in the 1960s,
particularly a high-profile one. Vernon Dahmer, Medgar
Evers, Harry Moore, Malcolm X, and countless others had
been killed for such defiance. Muhammad Ali, improbably,
but fortunately, outlived his vilification to become a revered icon, not only in the U.S., but throughout the world.

Nearly every black person I knew was in respectful
awe of Ali, except my mother, who, more than anything,

wanted black folks to be "normal." "I can't countenance anybody," she said, "who won't fight for his country."

Without any forewarning, Art announced he had accepted a position at Ohio University in Athens. *What?!* I had no idea he was looking for a job! I thought we were to be in A² until he finished his dissertation, which was still not completed. In researching this book, I learned that when we left Mt. Pleasant, Art had not resigned his job at Central Michigan, as I'd thought. Instead he took a year's leave of absence. While we were in Ann Arbor, he requested that CMU promote him from instructor to assistant professor. When the promotion was denied, he resigned. That was on May 30, 1967. It seemed he planned to return to CMU if they had promoted him, but when they didn't, Art accepted the offer from Ohio University (OU). More likely, he had the offer from Ohio University and made what he knew was a ridiculous demand from CMU —he was still ABD (all but dissertation)—so his resignation would be "justified."

I enjoyed living in Ann Arbor more than Art did. I would have been happy to remain there indefinitely, but Art had already left A² once for the rusticity of Mt. Pleasant. At the time, I thought his anxiety about my enchantment with brainy black men gave him a reason to leave Ann Arbor behind. Later, I learned that Art's primary reason for desiring rural locations was that he craved an outdoor life. I was shocked to learn he was enamored of hunting and fishing. His dream was to purchase land where he could do both whenever he wanted. I had never been hunting or fishing in my life and had no desire to do either. And, lord knows I didn't want to live out in the country! When I stopped allowing husbands and jobs to determine where I lived, I headed straight for Chicago, where I found all manner of intellectual, music, sports and cultural events. Any desire I had to be outdoors was satisfied by a morning walk along Lake Michigan, weather permitting. More than anything, I despised guns of any kind, and Art was collecting them!

In the summer of 1967, Art and I moved from Ann Arbor to Athens. At the time the University of Michigan had a student enrollment of 48,052, whereas Ohio University had 16,535 students. This was not the direction I wanted to go, but Art was adamant. I consoled myself that at least we would still be in an academic setting. As it turned out, this move I didn't want to make initiated a ground-breaking career for me in the study of America's marginalized ethnic groups, and led to my developing educational materials about these groups.

I no longer remember why, but before we moved we sold my car, the sleek Barracuda which was my first major purchase as a professional woman. Probably Art made an argument against the need for two cars, and I yielded in my hope of making the marriage "work." By keeping his car and selling mine, my independence was immediately curtailed. He would have more control over where I went, even if he didn't know what happened after I got there.

In 1804 Ohio University was the first institution of higher learning chartered in the Northwest Territory— the area that became the states of Ohio, Indiana, Illinois, Wisconsin and Michigan. Athens, with a 2009 population of twenty thousand or so, is a hilly, picturesque area. It's part of Appalachia, sixty-four miles southeast of the state capital in Columbus, and less than a hundred miles west of

Charleston, West Virginia. The Hocking River, a tributary of the Ohio, flows through the town, and OU has been referred to as "Harvard on the Hocking." In fact, several of the buildings on the College Green are the same Georgian architecture found in Harvard Yard.

The first black student, John Newton Templeton, graduated from Ohio University in 1828. Templeton was born into slavery in South Carolina around 1805. He was emancipated in 1813 at age eight by his "owner's" Last Will and Testament. After they were released from captivity, the family moved to Ohio. To cover his expenses at OU, Templeton lived and worked in the presidential residence of Robert G. Wilson. Templeton was the fourth African-American college graduate in America, and the first in the Midwest. He was arrested in Virginia in 1835 for teaching other black people to read and write. That arrest possibly contributed to his decision to leave the South and settle in Pittsburgh, where he became a teacher and principal of the city's first African School.

Athens also has the distinction of a historic connection to Booker T. Washington, the legendary co-founder and president of Tuskegee Institute (now University) in Alabama. Washington married his second wife Olivia Davidson in Athens in 1886. She is rarely acknowledged, but Davidson helped Washington establish Tuskegee and was an administrator there. They were married at her sister and brother-in-law's home. In 2008, the OU Department of African American Studies and the Athens County Historical Society and Museum placed a historical marker on the house.

In the period after the Civil War up through the early twentieth century Athens had a significant black community. Davidson's brother-in-law, Noah Elliott, was Athens' first African-American physician. Three African Americans were members of the university's board of trustees between 1885 and 1911. However, when we moved there in the late 1960s, aside from OU students and a few black faculty, Athens' black population was barely noticeable. In 2014, the black population in Athens County was estimated at 2.8%.

Art was hired as an assistant professor in the Department of Sociology and Anthropology. I was surprised to see that the chairman of his department, Benjamin Dennis, was from Liberia, a West African country. (It was yet another encounter that shattered my Indiana-bred assumptions about barriers to black attainment. In the three years since I left Indiana I'd had my first black professor, married a white man, and now found a black man chairing a department at a predominately white university. My decision to explore the world outside Indianapolis was a worthy idea.) Dr. Dennis's life was shaped by three continents—Africa, Europe, and North America. He was the son of a Liberian diplomat assigned to Germany. While he was growing up in Germany, he spent summers with his grandparents in Liberia. After 1950, he relocated to the United States where he earned a double Ph.D. in Sociology and Anthropology from Michigan State University in 1963.

We rented a partially furnished ranch-style home at 40 Graham Drive from an OU professor, David Levinson. He and his wife were departing for a sabbatical. For the first of the two years we lived there, we shared the house with their adult son, who occupied the basement. It was a lovely modern home with a fireplace in the living room, a dining room, two bedrooms, and a wood-paneled office/library. The large backyard included a bird-feeder and a wire suet cage, both of which I replenished regularly. It was a treat for me to observe and identify the different bird species—some regular diners, as well as flocks of colorful and unusual birds who stopped for a meal during their migrations. I was thrilled one day to see a huge red-headed pileated woodpecker rhythmically pounding one of the trees.

They asked me to take care of their copious flower garden and water the numerous houseplants, including a beautiful, large jade tree. I was completely inexperienced with succulent house plants and drowned the jade. The garden was a tapestry of various flowers; something was in bloom from early spring until the first freeze, including the most beautiful calla lilies I'd ever seen outside a florist's shop. I knew little about tending a flower garden, but did the best I could. The Levinson's undoubtedly had some retrieval to do when they returned home.

I had the leisure to garden and watch birds because, for the first time since I was thirteen years old, I did not have a job. To fill the vacant space in my days I enrolled in three courses at the university. I wanted to learn more about the continent of my ancestors and took two classes on Africa—one in the Geography Department on West Africa, and the other an anthropology class about Africans and Their Cultures. I took Basic Spoken French, simply because French was the only course I had ever flunked; I needed to prove I could master it. I was vindicated by earning an A! And I had a second black professor; Rene Sterlin, my French professor, was from Haiti. Taking classes with him or his American wife, Anne, I completed two years of French. It was fun taking courses just to learn stuff.

Not long after we moved in, Ruth Clearfield, a neighbor on Graham Drive, brought us a welcome wagon package. She was so convivial that we soon became friends.

Ruth and her husband Abe, a chemistry professor, were Jews like Art. They introduced us to their good friends, Ron and Arlene Williams, whom they knew because their children attended the same school. In addition to Art's department chair and my French teacher, there were three other black male professors at Ohio U. Three of the five were married to whites. Ron and Arlene were one of the two black couples. (Floyd and Yvonne Gaffney were the other one.) Ron, a professor in Hearing and Speech Sciences, had recently begun commuting to Ohio State University in Columbus to obtain his doctorate. I could see that Ron was more motivated than Art and would complete his Ph.D. quickly. Art had been ABD for nearly four years already. Ron finished in 1969 and Art in 1970. A few years later, Ron was president of Northeastern Illinois University.

Ruth was working on her bachelor's degree at OU, and when we were in the same French class we studied together. She was a marvelous gourmet cook and a meticulous housekeeper. Her oven gleamed, looking as if it were never used, but I knew better because she baked incredible desserts. I was inspired by Ruth and her recipes and challenged myself to cook a gourmet meal every day. That kept me entertained for a while, and Art's expanding waistline was proof of how much he enjoyed my experiments. But the domestic arts were never a keen interest of mine, so I started job hunting.

During the 1967 winter vacation Art and I planned a trip to Jamaica to visit his buddy and former U of M roommate, Richard Thelwell. We decided to stop in Miami on the way so that, after two years of marriage, I could meet the other members of Art's family. Except for Sharon, his younger sister, Art's family were all in Miami—his parents

Sol and Mimi, his sister Sunny, her husband Marvin, and their three children. The time lapse between our marriage and meeting his parents wasn't significant; Art wasn't close to his family. When we met, he hadn't seen them for three years. After Art told his parents we were coming for a visit, the family panicked about where we would stay in racially segregated Miami. It seemed that Art's parents' small one-bedroom apartment wouldn't comfortably accommodate us. I was told that Sunny asked her maid for names of black hotels, but found her suggestions unacceptable. After many telephone calls and much hand wringing, the family decided that Art and I would stay with Sunny and her family in their four-bedroom home. I won't speculate on why it took so long to find that rather obvious solution.

Sunny lived in a beautiful, spacious home with her husband, two teenage daughters, and a young son. One of the girls shared a room with her sister for the few days of our visit, freeing her room for our use. The sprawling one-story house was colorfully decorated and immaculate. With Vietra, the maid, changing bed linens and putting out fresh towels every day, it was like staying in a hotel. I felt for her having so much laundry to do, but she seemed happy with her job. The first morning we were there, being who I am, I slept later than everybody else. When I got out of bed, breakfast was over. Sunny sent me to the kitchen saying that Vietra would fix something for me. I saw bagels, pastries, and a pot of coffee on the kitchen counter and decided to help myself. Vietra walked in as I lifted the cover from the pastries.

"Please sit down. I'll take care of that."

"That's okay, I can do it." I'd been a maid, but never had one, so I was uneasy about being served, especially by an older black woman.

"No, no, no. I waited on everybody else, and I'm sure going to wait on you!" Vietra was emphatic with her melodic West Indian accent, and gently pushed me toward the table.

I smiled and sat down while she heated and plated a pastry and poured coffee. While I ate, she leaned against the counter and we chatted. Vietra, who looked to be forty-something, had emigrated from Trinidad, loved living in Miami, and enjoyed her job. She obviously relished serving me. Every time I ran into her during our visit, she gave me a little smile that seemed to say, "You go, girl!"

Sunny and her family were friendly, gracious, and seemingly comfortable with their dark-skinned houseguest. As I recall, Sol, Art's dad, didn't say much, but was polite without any special warmth or disdain. Art's mom seemed extremely nervous and never stopped talking, as if she was uncertain how to behave with a strange creature like me, but for all I knew, she was like that with everyone. Nobody was rude or insulting; I was at ease.

One day Art and I were out and about in Miami and passed a vendor selling hot knishes, a food I'd never heard of. Art bought a kasha knish—seasoned buckwheat groats baked in pastry—which he shared with me to see if I liked it. I loved it, and on another occasion, when we had dinner at his parents' apartment, Mimi served a kasha and pasta dish with garlic that I loved as well. I have been a kasha fan ever since. Also in Miami, for the first time I had a kosher hot dog garnished with sauerkraut. Yummmm!

On another occasion, Art, his brother-in-law, Marvin, and I were walking along a stretch of Miami Beach with the high-rise tourist hotels. I think we were on our way to meet Sunny to have dinner in some posh restaurant. It was clearly a place where I would never have been welcomed

Richard Thelwell

alone, nor did I see
any other black people
strolling the beach-
front. I was walking
between Art and Mar-
vin and noticed that
people kept staring
and smiling broadly
at us, not the reac-
tion Art and I usually
received. Art noticed
it as well and said, "They think you're Miriam Makeba."
Makeba was an internationally known South African
singer, actor, and civil rights activist who was popular at
the time. A black woman with short natural hair accompanied by two white men *had to be Makeba.* Any other black
woman in that setting would have been in uniform at work
in one of the hotels or restaurants.

After four nights and three days, we left Miami and
flew to Kingston, Jamaica. Richard and Linda, his white
American wife, met our plane. It was my first trip outside
the U.S. In 1967 passports were not required for travel
to the Caribbean; to re-enter the U.S. you needed only a
driver's license.

I loved nearly everything about Jamaica beginning
with the tropical climate—even plants without blooms
were colorful. Dazzling red poinsettias grew everywhere.
Some were so large, they looked like flowering trees. Many

of the plants we purchase for indoor decorative purposes in this country were growing casually all over the place in Jamaica. Unlike Midwestern humidity, however, the moisture in Jamaica was never dried out by winter heat. There was often a moldy smell in homes and businesses, sometimes faint, but in other places more pronounced. Richard said the humidity was one reason carpeting was not popular in Jamaica. I especially liked the languid pace and the indifferent attitude Jamaicans had about punctuality.

Most striking of all, though was that I had never been in a country where the majority of people were *black!* WOW! It was amazing. Everywhere I looked, black folk, and more black folk. We rarely saw people of European descent until Richard took us to the luxury hotels that catered to Jamaica's thriving tourist business. There, most of the guests were white, but the staff was black. No wonder Richard carried himself like he owned the world. He had not grown up surrounded by people telling him he was inferior because of his skin color. It was difficult for me to imagine what that must feel like.

I was put off, however, by the rigid class structure. I could see the deference Richard, and all of us received from other Jamaicans. And I noticed that families, who didn't appear to be materially well off, had several servants.

"Richard, I thought a black country would be more egalitarian, but if anything, class differences are more pronounced here than in the states."

"It's because we were a British colony for so long, and our minds and our economy are still colonized." Richard was not happy with the way his country functioned.

"I keep telling you. It's *capitalism,* not race, that creates inequities here and everywhere there's a capitalist system." Art pressed his point yet again.

He and Richard shared similar views on economics and politics, which no doubt had a lot to do with their friendship. It took a while for me to understand why Art was comfortable with Richard when most educated black men rattled him.

Black and white Americans are locked together in a largely unconscious cultural prison of suspicion, resentment, shame, and guilt. This construction, manufactured by hundreds of years of American slavery and racial subjugation, is built on the premise that people of European descent are inherently superior to people of African descent. Everyone, including blacks, is expected to operate as if that premise is correct. After World War II in the years leading up to the civil disobedience of the 1960s, we black folks became bolder about expressing our impatience with racial oppression. We became increasingly unwilling to accommodate white denial of American racism. Nor were we willing to continue cloaking our anger at the way we are treated. I was regularly chastised by whites, especially in the workplace, for being arrogant and/or having a "bad attitude." I knew this assessment meant they rejected my belief I was due the same respect and consideration they took for granted. In the second decade of the twenty-first century more people than ever of European descent are beginning to acknowledge the systemic assumption of white supremacy and its impact on everyone in this country.

People of African descent who immigrate to America are often educated and/or from the upper classes in their home countries, where whites are a decided minority. These empowered black folks have not been socialized to be wary of whites as American blacks have learned to be. Consequently, there is a different dynamic between these black immigrants and white Americans.

Although Richard was born into Jamaica's upper echelon, and his education abroad and government position kept him firmly in that class, his sentiments were decidedly with the masses who were, in many cases, desperately poor. He made sure we saw every aspect of Jamaica, including the appalling slums of Trenchtown and Jones Town. I was astounded to see people crowded together in ramshackle housing without indoor plumbing. It looked like a gigantic trash heap, but it was a residential area. In my reading, I'd seen occasional pictures of similar situations in the United States, but I had never personally witnessed such conditions.

Linda and Richard had household help who took care of their cooking, cleaning, and laundry.

"Do you pay your servants well?" I asked.

"I pay the going wage. Otherwise it would create dysfunction in the system. It won't change anything if I pay them more than everybody else. The way for me to help is to change the system." That made sense. I admired Richard and often wished I had met him *before* I married Art.

I saw one of their maids washing clothes on a scrub board like the one my mother had discarded for a wringer washing machine more than twenty years earlier. Then I understood why Vietra didn't mind doing laundry every day in Miami—she was using an automatic washer and dryer, rather than a scrub board and facing the frustration of drying clothes outside in humid weather.

One of the best meals we had in Jamaica was at what looked like a wooden shack on the beach, but in fact was a restaurant. We sat outside where most of the tables were set up. Richard suggested we order lobster.

"I don't like lobster," I responded. I had heard about

this supposed delicacy, but only eaten it once. Art ordered it at a fancy restaurant in Athens and I was excited to finally experience this choice food I'd heard people salivating about.

"Really? Why not?" Richard was surprised.

"It's tough and tastes like cardboard."

"Where did you have a tough lobster?"

"At this expensive restaurant in Athens."

Richard threw back his head and laughed hard, then said, "You need to try freshly-caught lobster before you decide you don't like it."

Richard was right, of course. We watched as the guys from the restaurant literally waded into the water and came back with our lobsters. The lobster was wonderfully tender and delicious, bearing no resemblance to the tasteless version of my first experience.

One evening the four of us were out having dinner and I mentioned that I had once worked as a maid. Richard refused to believe it! It was only after I answered several of his penetrating questions about my experience, that he was finally convinced. When I finished my story, Richard was quiet for a moment. Then he said, "That's what's great about America. Where else could a black servant girl get an education and marry a white professor? That would never happen here."

We met Richard's mother who lived in a large house with her husband, a British expatriate she married after Richard's dad, a government official, died. The grounds of the expansive house were awash in brightly colored bougainvillea. Mrs. Thelwell (I don't recall the name of her then-husband) was an attractive, haughty, light-skinned woman, probably with no more than a quarter of African ancestry. Richard was the only one of her three children living in Jamaica. Her light-skinned daughter lived in England with her British husband and their children. Her other son, Michael, was in the U.S. where he still resides. (More about him later.) Mrs. Thelwell showed us pictures of her grandchildren who looked as if they had no African ancestry at all. Richard said his mother loved to show off her white grandchildren.

I was struck by how sparsely furnished Mrs. Thelwell's home was. I was told that good furniture was difficult to come by in Jamaica since much of it was imported and consequently quite expensive.

Chapter 7

Making Demands

Power concedes nothing without a demand. It never has and it never will.

~ Frederick Douglass

Art and I returned to Athens in late December, and in early January 1968 I began work as a reference librarian at Ohio University's Chubb Library. I liked working the reference desk helping students and faculty. One day I found myself silently fantasizing about a good-looking black graduate student who spent a lot of time studying in the library. I was horny and there were no single black men around to let my imagination run wild about. I had concluded that Art's dictum about intellectuals not needing sex was bullshit, but I hadn't yet figured out how or what to do about it. So far as I was concerned, sex was a major joy, a necessity, even. I had just turned thirty, and according to some researchers, was approaching my sexual prime. Prime or not, I was so desperate to have sex that I began sizing up the black male students. Because I knew there was no way *any* student would be able to keep secret the fact that he'd been with a professor's wife; especially the black wife of a white professor, I never acted on that insane thought.

I'm not sure how (or even why?) the subject came up, but Art was shocked when I told him that if we had children, they'd be black.

"How can that be? No, that's not right! How could my son be black?"

"Don't you know about the 'one drop' rule? Slaveholders declared that any child born to an enslaved woman was their property. And, of course, only black folk could be enslaved, so even if the slaver fathered the child, the child had to be deemed 'black,' to be added to his property."

"But slavery's over and done with. We can't still be going by that ridiculous idea."

"Well, we are. Clearly, you're not paying attention. Whenever a black person and a white person have a child, the child is always classified as black. It doesn't matter what they look like. Look at Sammy Davis Jr. and May Britt. Their daughter will not be 'white,' no matter what she looks like. Or, look at Massachusetts Senator Ed Brooke. He's no darker than you are, but at least one of his ancestors is African, no matter how far back, so he and his offspring are forever black, unless one of them decides to ignore the one-drop rule."

"This is crazy. Unbelievable." Art didn't take my word for it. He did his own research, and when it corroborated everything I'd told him, he added it to the syllabus for one of his classes. But he was still outraged that the privileges of his white skin could not be passed on to any children we might have. That's *not* what caused his impotence, however; we had this conversation long after our sex life had passed away.

Many of the children fathered by the slavers, were physically indistinguishable from their half-siblings in the big house, but they could not be "white" because American slavery was constructed on the notion of white supremacy. Only folks of African descent were enslaved. "Superior" people of European descent were not enslaved. Ironically, that "superior" genetic material, no matter how well-born, could not supersede even a "drop" of the powerful African bloodline.

The Transatlantic Slave Trade was abolished in 1808, thereby ending the *legal* importation of Africans. For more than half a century, when a slaver wanted to increase his estate, he could either purchase from another slaver, buy illegally, or "breed." Breeding meant forcing young black women to have sex with the slaver's male "property." Or, the slaver would rape and impregnate the women himself. "Breeding" was legal, as well as being more cost-effective than his other options.

African biological dominance continues to be significant in the twenty-first century. In 2009 Barack Obama's maternal heritage was considered inconsequential when he was inaugurated as America's first *black* president. African Americans have always welcomed these additions to our population because, in a country that diligently counts and classifies its citizens by their "race," as variously defined by the Bureau of the Census, it is important for each "race" to grow their numbers. The larger your population, the more clout you presumably have.

Although I was successful working at the OU library Reference Desk, I was transferred to another department. Allegedly, the library had a policy requiring each librarian to periodically rotate to another department. I was told the policy was meant to help librarians become knowledgeable about all library functions. Considering that I worked at the library less than six months, my "rotation" came up rather quickly. I was moved to the cataloging department within weeks after I was hired. Did someone complain about a black person working in a visible position interacting with the public? At the time, I didn't question the change. My stint at the reference desk was indeed helpful in determining how a book should be cataloged, as well as suggesting subject categories appropriate for the title. As I write about my life experiences, it is fascinating to see that several attempts to demean me because of my gender and/or African ancestry have contributed to the breadth of my knowledge. America's endemic racism has, indeed, fertilized my growth.

On November 30, 1967, not long before I began my job at the library, Eugene McCarthy, a U.S. senator from Minnesota, announced he would oppose President Lyndon Johnson for the Democratic Party presidential nomination. Along with millions of Americans, Senator McCarthy was tired of the escalating war in Vietnam. He was running to give voice to those who wanted to end the war. Art and I donated money to his campaign. We also went to hear him speak when he visited OU's campus in January, accompanied by Paul Newman, a popular actor and former OU student. McCarthy was admired by peace activists and the young people who didn't want to be drafted into the war. The demonstrations against the war were increasing in size and frequency, giving McCarthy the support he needed to challenge the President. After McCarthy won forty-two percent of the vote in the New Hampshire primary, Senator Robert Kennedy, brother of President John Kennedy, who had been slain five years earlier, also decided to enter the competition for the Democratic nomination. After Senator Kennedy announced his run, President Johnson decided to step aside, perhaps sensing that running against another Kennedy would be a lost cause. John Kennedy had defeated Johnson for the Democratic nomination in 1960, and the Kennedy name became golden after he was assassinated. On March 31, the president stated, "I shall not seek, and I will not accept, the nomination of my party for another term as your President."

Without Johnson in the Oval Office, I figured that any follow-through on the Kerner Commission was doomed. In July 1967, President Johnson had appointed an eleven-member National Advisory Commission on Civil Disorders, usually referred to by the name of its chairman, Otto Kerner Jr., former governor of Illinois. Johnson asked the Commission to find out why urban blacks were exploding in anger and destroying property. The president wanted the commission to analyze the "specific triggers" for the eruptions and suggest remedies. The report famously warned: that the U. S. was "moving toward two societies, one black, one white—separate and unequal." So far as I, and most blacks, were concerned, we had *always* lived in two separate and unequal societies, both before and after the abolition of slavery. The commission's recommendations for federal action to correct the situation were never implemented.

Four days after the president's announcement that he would not seek office again, and three months into my library gig, Dr. Martin Luther King Jr. was murdered on Thursday, April 4, 1968 in Memphis, Tennessee.

Nothing was the same after that.

Art and I were in bed watching television when the program was interrupted with the announcement of King's assassination. My immediate reaction was, "The bastards finally did it! I knew they would kill him!"

"They" were the FBI's COINTELPRO (the Counter Intelligence Program) created to destroy protest groups

that J. Edgar Hoover deemed a "national security risk."
COINTELPRO had become bold to the point of obscenity,
infiltrating and disrupting every organization working to
end the oppression of black people. COINTELPRO opera-
tives had locked up numerous activists on bogus charges,
and created a climate that encouraged murdering—or had
their own people kill—those who opposed racial oppression, including Medgar Evers, Malcolm X, and now King.

I was angry that Dr. King was violently assassinated,
but privately felt relieved for him. His strategy of peaceful
resistance was losing ground, especially with young people
who were tired of turning the other cheek. It seemed that
no matter how many cheeks were offered, all were met
with brutal slaps, water hoses, dogs, or death. We younger
folk were more inclined toward the SNCC leadership of
Stokely Carmichael and H. Rap Brown, or Huey Newton
and Bobby Seale of the Black Panther Party (BPP), based
in Oakland, California. I had a subscription to the BPP
newspaper, *The Black Panther*, and read it eagerly.

"Well," I told Art, "now King will be remembered as a
martyr rather than a failed leader."

King's approach to resolving racial discrimination
had worked sporadically in the South, but been patently
ineffective in northern cities, which exploded again in a
convulsive rage that the "King of Peace" was dead. Pre-
dictably, he had been killed by a white man, or more
accurately, by the powers exploiting the racially hostile
climate. I watched the television clip where Senator Kennedy, campaigning in my home town of Indianapolis, announced that King had been assassinated. Friends told me
that some in the audience cheered the news. Two months
later we were staggered when Kennedy, himself, was assassinated in California.

I had not expected Kennedy's assassination, but why not? After all, this country was erected on a foundation of violence, beginning with invaders from Europe killing and removing the original inhabitants to lay claim to the land. America ardently embraces guns and wars, and violently opposes peaceful dissent. Deaths by firearms in this country can't be surprising because they occur with such regularity. (During my research, I was surprised to see, in a departure from contemporary ideology, that in May 1968, James Kilpatrick, conservative journalist and white supremacist, was pleading for better gun control in his syndicated column. Kilpatrick was possibly inspired to make this plea by the widely-publicized images of armed members of the Black Panther Party marching into a session of the California legislature in 1967.) The jolt I felt over Robert Kennedy's murder no doubt had more to do with the idea that *two high-profile men* working to make things better for oppressed people were killed within a space of sixty-one days. I suppose they were both "threats to national security."

Despite the FBI's murderous efforts, blacks forged ahead. Every obstacle we overcame added to our strength and determination. I thought about Sterling Brown's 1932 poem, "Strong Men."

> *They dragged you from homeland,*
> *They chained you in coffles,*
> *They huddled you spoon-fashion in filthy hatches,*
> *They sold you to give a few gentlemen ease....*

> *They point with pride to the roads you built for them,*
> *They ride in comfort over the rails you laid for them....*

You sang:
> *Me an' muh baby gonna shine, shine*
> *Me an' muh baby gonna shine, shine*
> The strong men keep a-comin' on
> The strong men git stronger....

One thing they cannot prohibit—
> The strong men...coming on
> The strong men gittin' stronger.
> Strong men....
> Stronger....

After King was killed, OU students had a memorial rally to pay tribute to Dr. King and to vent their wrath. There were about 4,000 in attendance, including Art and me. James Steele, Chairman of OU's Black Student Action Coordinating Committee (BSACC), thundered, "The King is Dead!" "The King is Dead!" "The King of Peace is Dead!" The crowd, both black and white, joined in the chant. We were not only grieving, but also affronted that King, the advocate of peace, had been violently murdered. Steele continued, "Like a true king, he lived his life for his people. Who among us, white or black, has the fortitude to preach nonviolence and face the consequences as he did?"

After the rally, about "two hundred grieving students and faculty members staged a sit-in at the corner of Court and Union streets." Police wanted to remove them by force, but OU Vice President James Whalen and Steele talked them down, precluding what undoubtedly would have been a violent confrontation.

At the time, there were about a thousand black students in OU's enrollment of nearly 17,000. Vernon R. Alden, university president since 1962, had encouraged a more inclusive student body and opened the dormitories to all students. A nondiscriminatory enrollment policy was publicized in the 1964 catalog. Betty Hollow, author of *Ohio University 1804-2004*, wrote, "There were more African American students on campus than there had ever been, but they remained a community within a community, depending on themselves for academic and emotional support, and for most of their limited social life." (When I read this, it reminded me of my experience as a student at Indiana University. We thought of ourselves as a "small black college surrounded by a large white college.")

Because black students had to fend for themselves, the BSACC had proposed a plan for Ohio University to recognize and celebrate Negro History Week in February 1968, a first for the university. OU supported their proposal, and celebrities speaking and performing on campus that week were Floyd McKissick, National Chairman of CORE; Dick Gregory, comedian and activist; John Wooten, a football player for the Cleveland Browns and one of Ali's supporters; and Motown's Smokey Robinson and the Miracles.

Students built on the proud spirit generated by their celebration of Negro History Week by preparing a theatrical production titled "A Hand is on the Gate." The title comes from this verse of the poem "Southern Mansion" written by Arna Bontemps.

> *The years go back with an iron clank,*
> *A hand is on the gate,*
> *A dry leaf trembles on the wall.*
> *Ghosts are walking.*

Dr. Floyd Gaffney of OU's Theater Department, had seen an off-Broadway production of "A Hand is on the Gate," in New York, and introduced the concept to his students. Gaffney directed the performance, my good friend, Lois McGuire, was Gaffney's assistant director, and I helped students identify and locate material they could use. Lois was a black graduate student in speech and theater working on her master's degree. Rehearsals were held at the Baptist Church, and because Lois had a car, she provided transportation for some of the students. "A Hand is on the Gate" ran May 9-12, 1968, and offered an atypically accurate account of African American history through poetry, song, and dance.

It was a moving, magnificent presentation, and a huge success—the talk of the campus. The students were talented, well-rehearsed, and obviously grateful for the opportunity to be involved in something created by, about, and for them. Watching them perform, I was proud to see a public representation of black people that was inspiring and empowering. Not everybody was as excited as I was, but a favorable review in the *Athens Messenger* did describe it as a "Unique lesson in history."

Although Ohio University had graduated Templeton, its first black student, in 1828, their first black faculty member was not hired for another one hundred thirty-four years. E. Curmie Price joined the faculty of the English Department in 1963; however, when I became a part of that department in 1968, he was no longer there. Several other prospective black faculty turned down offers from OU because they were unable to find "satisfactory housing" in the area. (Art and I later encountered similar difficulties with the availability of housing in Athens.)

After Dr. King was killed, the BSACC resolved to confront the OU administration about some of these racial deficits, especially the sparse numbers of black faculty and staff on campus. Before they approached the university, they called for a blacks-only meeting to receive input from all interested African Americans on campus.

As I prepared to attend that meeting, Art said he was going with me.

"No, you're not! It's a meeting for *blacks only*. Why would you even suggest such a thing?"

Art was equally vehement. "I've been working for civil rights longer than you have. I'm going to the meeting."

"What?!" I screamed at him. "You've been doing what? Are you kidding me? I was *born* into…!"

Art wasn't listening to me; he was making his point.

"The students know I'm married to you. There's no way *I* should be left out of this meeting."

Oh, so that's what I am: his entrée to blackness! His attending the meeting was not debatable so far as I was concerned. I spoke calmly. "I'm not saying you can't go, Art. You just can't go *with me*."

He knew he would not be admitted if he wasn't with me, so he dug deep to justify his absurd idea. "Do you *hear* what you're saying? How would you feel if there were a whites-only meeting and I refused to take you?"

"Are you insane? Why would I *want* to go to a whites-only meeting!? Besides, that wouldn't be anything new, I've spent most of my life being excluded from 'whites only' places. There is nothing, *nothing* you can say that will make me take you to this meeting with me."

As noted earlier, three of the five black faculty members at OU were in mixed marriages—all black men with white women. Art and I were an anomaly. He was the only white male faculty member married to a black person. No one seemed particularly interested in these unusual (at that time) marriages until Dr. King was assassinated. In the emotionally charged atmosphere after King's murder, students were radicalized and more vociferous about their pride in being black. A few of them had already taunted me with "talking black and sleeping white." This jeer was also applied to any black student who was dating a white person, especially if they were also involved in protests and demonstrations. If I brought Art to this unprecedented call for black unity, my credibility would be shredded.

Art, acting out of his usual presumptuousness that he could go where he pleased, was adamant about not being left out. He accused me of being racist if I went along with their blacks-only edict when some whites, including him, of course, had given so much to the cause for racial justice. Then he brought up Andrew Goodman, Michael Schwerner, and Viola Liuzzo, white civil rights workers who were killed in Mississippi and Alabama in 1964 and 1965 respectively. I caved to that point, mostly because if we continued arguing about it, I would have missed the meeting altogether. I have never been as ashamed as I was walking into that meeting with him. He was the only white person there. Making the matter even more soul-crushing, I was called out and asked to explain why I brought Art to an all-black meeting. I was mortified! I have totally repressed how I "justified" bringing Art with me. Whatever I said, it convinced them to let us stay.

"I told you it would be okay for me to attend the meeting. It worked out fine!" Art gloated about his "victory." I was too furious to speak. "It" hadn't worked out; *I'd had to work it out* in a public humiliation. He didn't care how I felt, so long as he got what he wanted.

I had known for a while that our marriage was in trouble. That night, I knew *for sure* that my venture across the color line was doomed. When my first marriage ended unexpectedly, I had to borrow money from my sister and her husband to return to school. I would not leave empty-handed this time. I transferred money from our checking account into a savings account, and began to prepare for my getaway. I was aware that if Art knew I planned to leave, he would resist in every way possible. I was particularly concerned about the possibility of his grabbing a gun during one of his raging tantrums.

The black students rocked the campus by presenting the administration with a list of their demands. The demands included, among other things, additional black faculty, especially for courses on black history and culture; the establishment of a Black Studies Department; a black vice-president of the university; and scholarship money for black students. They promised to sit-in at the administration building until their demands were met. A copy of the list was sent to the campus newspaper so everybody on campus would know what their goals were. President Alden's initial response was that he did not respond to ultimatums. Alden's stance had no impact on the students, who continued their vigil in the hallway outside his office while others marched with signs in front of the building.

A few faculty members were in support of the student effort, and about fifteen of them, including four of the five black faculty, met with Alden to express their views. Art was initially involved with this group, but withdrew because he said they were "spineless." I worked in the library, so I was "staff," not faculty, and wasn't a part of the group.

After I became faculty, I thought I would be included; instead I continued to learn about their sporadic meetings after the fact. That hurt. As usual, men advocating for "equal rights," excluded women from their deliberations. Despite the number of women who made significant and lasting contributions to the civil rights movement, those organizations—NAACP, SCLC, CORE, SNCC—were notorious for their male chauvinism.

I never confronted the male faculty about excluding me, largely because I felt I was more effective working directly with the students. I advised them on strategy, helped to buy food for those who missed dining hall meals, and encouraged them not to give up. I also passed along everything I could learn from Art and other sympathetic faculty and staff about how their actions were being received by the administration. With students in the hallway outside the president's office and picketing outside the administration building from the moment it opened until it closed, the campus could focus on little else. Black students came from nearby colleges to help and to provide bodies for the protest. This happened at Ohio University a year before the Cornell University black student protests received national media coverage, but four years after the University of California at Berkeley's Free Speech Movement.

This is my recollection of that historic time. Alden described it another way, "Black students at Ohio University presented their demands in a dignified, constructive manner." Perhaps, the black students' efforts seemed "dignified" in comparison to the rock-throwing demonstrations and near-riots that other grievances brought on during Alden's presidency. Nonacademic employees went on strike to get the university to recognize their union. Students wanted more freedom, especially concerning the requirement that they live in university-approved housing until age twenty-three. They also wanted more information and input on how the fees they paid were spent. Women were upset about overcrowded dorms and their restricted hours. Betty Hollow summed it up, saying, "[T]he mood of the campus was changing. One group after another seemed to catch the revolutionary spirit of the times and protest the status quo." Alden observed, "[There was] sharp, often savage, criticism of university leadership by editors of the *Post*." The *Post* was the award-winning Ohio University student newspaper.

Steele expressed the BSACC goal: "I believe the University should prepare a student to function in a multiracial world. It does not. …Our objective in all of our activities to date has been to take our militancy and use it in a constructive manner in terms of education."

Some of Steele's admirers called him "Prophet." I often heard students refer to him by that moniker. Months later, after some of their demands had been met, and a few of the more active members of the BSACC, including Steele, had titled positions in the newly established Black Studies Institute, I heard some snickering that his nickname was spelled, P-R-O-F-I-T.

Years later, James Gilliam, an OU student at the time, wrote about how he was affected by the upheavals. "My life and that of many other African-Americans was also deeply touched by the assassination of Martin Luther King, Jr.… There were riots on many college campuses, and mine was no exception. I had not yet resigned from the ROTC program and, therefore, I had access to some of the antiquated World War II weapons and ammunition we trained with. My refusal to get the keys to the armory and pass them to angry African-American students made my life difficult."

James "Prophet" Steele speaking at M. L. King Memorial, April 7, 1968
Courtesy of Ohio University Photographer Collection Ohio University Archives

A couple of weeks after the sit-in began, Alden announced that the university would add courses in black
literature and history and hire blacks to teach the new
courses. Purportedly, Alden made the decision about the
university's new direction "in consultation with students
and faculty and to honor the work of Martin Luther King,
Jr." In other words, the student action had no bearing on
his decision. The following year, in April 1969, President
Alden pledged $250,000 for a Black Studies Institute (BSI).

The 1969-70 OU Bulletin said the BSI was established
to "encourage students to develop individual perspectives
concerning the role of the black man in contemporary
society and to train action intellectuals —both black and
white — to be agents of change in their respective com-
munities. In its programs, the degree-granting institute
serves a dual function: it provides an academic framework
for studying the black experience historically, culturally,

socially, economically and politically, and it gives the black student at Ohio University an opportunity to develop a sense of identity through programs and services geared to his particular needs."

At the end of the 1968-69 academic year, Alden returned to Boston, where he had been at the Harvard School of Business, to take a position as Chairman of the Boston Company, a financial institution. In an online history of Alden's establishment of the university's Ohio Fellows Program, I found the following statement. "Alden led the University through notoriously tempestuous times. There were student protests over crowding, women's hours, parietal rules, and the prohibition of alcohol on campus, and there were labor problems and strikes by non-academic campus workers—and all of this against the background of the war in Vietnam." In keeping with this country's usual tradition of deleting African American contributions from written histories, the pivotal changes that resulted from the efforts of black students are missing from this account.

Chapter 8

Choosing New Possibilities

*In every moment of our existence, we are in that field
of all possibilities where we have access to an infinity
of choices.*

~ Deepak Chopra

After Alden's announcement that additional black
faculty would be hired, Dr. Wells, Chairman of the English
Department, called to ask if I would like to teach three sections of freshman composition focusing on black literature.

Yes, I would!

"This will be a volunteer position…"

"Volunteer? Why won't I get paid?" He knew I
worked full-time at the library. Did he expect me to quit
a paying job and *volunteer* to prepare for and teach three
college classes!?

"Professor's wives often volunteer at the university doing a variety of things, including teaching a class or two."

"I'll have to think about this and get back to you." I had
not expected to be among those added to the ranks of black
faculty, but being asked to teach without pay felt insulting.
I was exhilarated at the prospect of teaching black lit, but
I was not going to do it without being paid! What a disappointment. Why did he expect me to do it for nothing?

Wells wanted a response as soon as possible because
the Fall Quarter was just weeks away.

Art and I talked about Wells' proposition, and Art agreed it was preposterous.

Professor's wives volunteer! That may have been fine for *some women*, but I did not think of myself as *a professor's wife*. I had been working and getting *paid* since I was thirteen. Not being employed had never occurred to me—or to most black women. For us the goal was to obtain the training or education to *maximize* our earning potential, not to find a job where you didn't get *paid!* Some professors' wives may have been willing to be exploited that way, but I wasn't going for it.

Art asked, "Do you want to do it?"

"I'd love to do it; otherwise, where will students learn about black literature?"

I knew what Art's salary was as an assistant professor, and he told me what the starting salary was for a beginning OU instructor. "Call him back and tell him what you want."

I called Wells and told him I'd be happy to teach freshman comp, if it ever became a salaried position. He asked what kind of salary I was interested in. Remembering what happened with my first job offer after college, I asked for an amount above beginning instructor pay and slightly below Art's salary. Wells agreed on the spot! Obviously, the money was available; but why pay for something you can get for nothing? Once I thought about it, I realized I was one of very few black adults in town with a college degree who wasn't already teaching at the university. It was too late in the year to recruit professors from elsewhere. He had little choice.

Nearly all departments, including Botany, Economics, Geography, and Philosophy required their majors to take English Composition classes. Consequently, there were numerous sections with a variety of "themes." The OU course bulletin for 1968-69 divided the themes as either "literary" or "contemporary issues." These offerings were described as "Modern themes and problems which find expression in literature and thought of the 20th century. Guidance in critical thinking, reading and writing about those themes and problems."

The English department had freshman comp classes with a "black literature" theme before I started teaching. I examined that reading list and decided to make a new one for my classes. The existing list included the novels *Light in August* and *Go Down Moses* by William Faulkner and *Passage to India* by E. M. Forster, as well as other titles. There were only two books on the list by African American authors. They were biographies—Claude Brown's *Manchild in the Promised Land* and *The Autobiography of Malcolm X* with Alex Haley.

I decided to create a reading list of black authors. I resigned from the library. That summer I read and did research in preparation for teaching my first classes. I was pleasantly surprised to discover that the university library had an historic, but dusty, collection of books by African American writers, including many titles that had been out of print for decades. I put several of those books on reserve for my classes. For the student reading list, however, I needed currently available books, preferably in paperback.

I knew the students, like me, were products of an educational system that ignored the history and literature of black Americans, except perhaps for a paragraph or two on slavery. I wanted to give students an overview of our history through literature. I chose the following novels to read in this order: *Black Thunder* by Arna Bontemps, a fictionalized account of an actual rebellion against slavery, originally published in 1936 and reissued in 1968; *Jubilee* by Margaret Walker, about her forebears' trials and triumphs after the Civil War, published in 1966; *Autobiography of an Ex-Colored Man* by James Weldon Johnson, the story of a black man passing for white during the post-Reconstruction era and the beginning of the twentieth century, originally published in 1912; and Ralph Ellison's acclaimed classic, *Invisible Man*. Ellison's novel follows a nameless black man who moves out of the South during the 1930s-1940s to the industrial, urban North. *Invisible Man* has remained in print since it was initially published in 1952. I also added James Baldwin's *Go Tell It on the Mountain*, published in 1953. Baldwin's novel presents an earlier view of coming of age in Harlem that contrasts with that in the biographies of Brown and Malcolm X, both published in 1965, and whose books I retained on my revised list. Art scheduled his classes on Mondays and Wednesdays; I decided to hold mine on Tuesdays and Thursdays, no earlier than 10 a.m.

That summer of 1968 while I was preparing to teach, Richard Thelwell came to the U.S., probably to visit his brother, but he also stopped in Athens to see us for a couple of days. I was excited to have a virile black man in the house and greeted him warmly, offering every courtesy I could think of. I flirted outrageously, giving him a facial and a haircut, although I had little experience doing either, though I did cut Art's hair regularly. I just wanted to be close to Richard, a desire driven no doubt by my sexual deprivation. Art didn't seem to notice, or if he did, he never mentioned it. He and Richard had their usual lively arguments about politics.

Four years later in the summer of 1972, I made a second trip to Jamaica with my new love. Although we had not been in touch, I was able to track Richard down because he was well known in Kingston. That was the year the People's National Party, led by Michael Manley, won the country's election moving Jamaican politics to the left. Richard was thrilled with what seemed to be fresh and promising possibilities for his homeland. After I located him, we arranged to meet, and for the first time talked one-on-one. We were both in new relationships, this time with black folks, and in fact, I was expecting a baby. We related easily and candidly about our prior marriages and how we had evolved.

I asked, "Did you know I had a crush on you back then?"

He smiled and said, "I didn't think you were trying to hide it!"

In addition to working for the Jamaican government, Richard was managing a Rasta music group called the Mystic Revelation. They were about to take a chartered flight to perform at a Caribbean Festival of the Arts, Carifesta '72, taking place in Georgetown, Guyana. Richard invited us to go with them. He also arranged seats for us on the plane, and housing in the performers' village. It was an unexpected and glorious adventure. I heard steel drums for the first time; we were introduced to all kinds of brilliant music from all over the Caribbean. We met people from several countries, and somehow communicated with them, including those who did not speak English, the only language we knew.

❖ ❖ ❖

I still treasure the colorful gold pin given to each Carifesta participant.

The Fall Quarter 1968 opened on September 23, and I became the first black woman hired to teach at Ohio University. Several of the students who had organized, or been active in the demonstrations, enrolled in one or the other sections of my class. I was keenly disappointed when I learned they had no interest in reading the books on my list. They often repeated some of Malcolm X's rhetoric and liked being seen with his autobiography, but few had read the book. These young men preferred to spend class time denouncing whites for abuses heaped on Americans of African descent. And they believed their political activities had earned them an "A" in my class. They insisted there was no need to read books about the black experience because they were "living it."

These students, and others who looked up to them, could not be convinced they had anything to learn by reading, discussing, and writing about the books on my list. The students I had diligently supported were indignant at the suggestion that they needed information to go with their activism. The university had acceded to many of their demands, so obviously, they knew what they were doing! One student activist who rarely attended class and never took a test or wrote a paper, became angry and threatening when I gave him a D, and indeed it was a *gift* because I chose not to flunk him. When the next quarter began, the make-up of my classes changed. The word had spread that I required *all* my students to read the material and prepare for class. A couple of white men were also teaching sections of "black lit." These "liberal" instructors rewarded black students for venting their anger and castigating whites in class. (We still refer to that kind of patronizing behavior as the "racism of low expectations.") I was the only black person teaching freshman comp at the time, but my classes immediately changed from a largely black enrollment to having only a few black students. Not surprisingly, the prospect of an easy "A" from the other instructors was a lure for lots of students.

The good news was, that the students who signed up for my classes after that—both black and white—wanted to learn and knew there would be no venting and chastising.

I had found my calling, or perhaps, more accurately, my calling had found me.

Books were my first love. I had been reading since before I started school. By age nine or so, I had read all the books in the children's section of our neighborhood library. With a note to the librarian from my mom, who believed so fervently in books and the written word that she never censored her children's reading, I received permission to read any book I wanted. I was excited to have all the library's books available to me. In addition to this largesse, my father brought home books by black authors decades before they were commonly available in bookstores. As a result, I read Richard Wright's *Black Boy* when it was first published in 1945. I was eight-years-old. (When I read it again as an adult, I realized how much of the book I hadn't understood, but I had enjoyed reading it as a child, anyway.) Other black authors I read early on were Edwin Embree, Shirley Graham, Langston Hughes and Frank Yerby. Having a job that *required* me to read the work of black writers felt like the heavens had opened to bless me. That I would also introduce young people to these books and guide them in their interpretations meant that, like Br'er Rabbit, I had been tossed into my own briar patch!

My students were curious about what black folks had said about our history and experiences because they had only seen or heard the perspective of Americans of European descent. I was excited and inspired by their interest; however, the first time I gave an exam, only three or four students out of thirty or so passed. Those results made me question my effectiveness as an instructor. I asked the students why the exam had baffled them. It seemed that not many of them had understood what I considered important for them to retain. My primary task was to help improve their writing skills, but I had an additional goal to impart information about African American history and culture during that process. I threw out those exam results and started over.

In subsequent classes, I passed out the final exam on the first day of class and asked the students to answer as much as they could. The first time I checked these initial exams to see how much they already knew, I was shocked by the answer to one question. I had asked them to briefly identify Booker T. Washington, Marcus Garvey, Frederick Douglass, Martin Luther King Jr. and W.E.B. DuBois. The *only* one they all could identify was King, and only a few of them recognized *any* of the others. I thought they would be familiar with Washington and Douglass, but most had no idea who they were. I had books on reserve at the library for additional reading. These were books from which they could select a topic for their term paper. I added *Up from Slavery* by Washington and *Narrative of the Life of Frederick Douglass: An American Slave* to the reserved books.

For the final exam, I rearranged the same questions they had at the beginning, and presented them again. Already knowing what I considered important helped the students do better on their tests. I hope they also actually learned a few things.

I spent lots of time grading the short papers they

wrote regularly; it was, after all, a composition course. My greatest challenge was that some of the students, especially those from larger urban areas like Cleveland and Pittsburgh, had little understanding of sentence structure, grammar, and punctuation, let alone how to do library research, use a dictionary, or compose a paper. Like me, they had not been taught these things in high school. (In the gifted English classes I was enrolled in at my high school, we read "classic" literature and wrote papers about what we read. There was no instruction in the mechanics of writing. I recall one English teacher, Mr. Moffat, who would punch a hole in our papers when he found an error. Once the paper had three holes, he pronounced it too raggedy to read. That meant the student had to re-write the paper. I was proud that Mr. Moffat had only punched one hole in one of my papers one time. What I knew about writing, I learned from my constant reading.)

For lots of college students, composition classes are their introduction to writing. I suppose that's why these are required courses at most colleges. I had some students who were competent writers, but they were nearly always from suburban areas or smaller cities. An indifferent education in urban schools has been around for a very long time. I worked with several diligent students individually and allowed them to re-write their papers following my corrections, if they wanted to improve their grade. A few of them did; one young man repeatedly.

I was part of the English Department faculty at the same time as Daniel Keyes, author of the popular book, *Flowers for Algernon*. I read Keyes' book, and went to see *Charly*, the movie adaptation, which won an Academy Award for Cliff Robertson in the title role. As is often the case, the book was much better than the movie. David

Hostetler was another nationally known artist at OU while I was there. He was a professor of sculpture who worked in elm wood and bronze. All his sculptures were of women. Hostetler said, "For me woman is the thing...My thing— my meditation." I would like to have owned one of his magnificent works, but they were much too expensive for our budget. I met both men, but didn't get to know either of them.

I got to know another well-known figure from OU a little better. Clarence Page was an undergraduate student at OU while I was there, although not in any of my classes. We met years later when I was living in Chicago where I launched my publishing imprint. Page was working for *The Chicago Tribune*, where he is still employed as a nationally syndicated columnist, and a senior member of the *Tribune*'s editorial board. He is also an author, and the recipient of two Pulitzer prizes. Because of the intense activism at OU while he was there, Page referred to the university as "The Berkeley of the backwoods."

My experience teaching at Ohio University led to my life's work. I continued to study African American literature and subsequently taught at other colleges and universities. I had to be creative to acquire the knowledge I needed because there were no Black Studies programs or departments at that time. Fortunately, I was a trained librarian and familiar with black authors because I'd been reading them since I was a child. My first formal instruction in African American literature came after I moved to California in 1970. I was a graduate student in English at California State University, Hayward, but I enrolled in both of Charles Matthews' undergraduate Black Literature courses. Eighteen months later, as a student in the English doctoral program at Stanford University, I convinced my Nineteenth Century American Literature professor to let me study black writers whose work paralleled his reading list of white writers. For every novel, essay collection, biography, or oration on his list, I identified a nineteenth century African American writer in the same genre. On his essay exams and for the term paper assignment, I wrote about the authors I had read. He gave me an "A" in the course, although he admitted he had no knowledge of the material I was referencing. He also told me he would never again teach that course without including African American writers.

I didn't know it at the time, but while I was preparing to teach my first classes, Nathan Hare, was writing his "Conceptual Proposal for a Department of Black Studies." Hare was in the vanguard of the movement insisting that universities install a course of study on the experiences of African Americans. Henry Louis Gates Jr., today's preeminent historian of the African Diaspora, and Director of the Hutchins Center for African and African American Research at Harvard University, was a teenager when I started teaching at Ohio University.

Dr. Hare had gained national notoriety for being fired as a professor of sociology at Howard University, an HBCU (Historically Black College or University). Hare put his professorship in jeopardy by publicly declaring that a black university, rather than imitating white universities, should be relevant to the black community and its needs.

Although a few HBCU's were founded above the Mason-Dixon Line before the Civil War, most of them were established after the war ended. Tens of thousands of blacks for whom education had been forbidden, were eager to attend school once they were free to do so. Schools were opened throughout the South: Shaw University in 1865 in Raleigh, North Carolina; in 1866 Fisk in Nashville, Tennessee; and in 1867, Morehouse in Atlanta, and Howard University in Washington, D.C. Hampton in Virginia was the exception; it was opened in 1861, the year the Civil War began.

I settled into a pleasant routine with my teaching. Classes and office hours on Tuesdays and Thursdays; on Mondays and Wednesdays quiet time at home to grade papers and prepare for classes. When I needed to, I'd also grade papers over the weekend.

During the winter break, Art and I attended his department's Christmas party. Like many young blacks in the sixties, I was taking pride in my African heritage and no longer concerned that my appearance or behavior might disturb the people who think of themselves as white. I reveled in Stokely Carmichael's call for Black Power and welcomed the Nation of Islam's exhortation that blacks look to themselves for approval and acceptance, rather than to whites. All my life I had been instructed not to do anything that might lend credence to negative white ideas of who we were. This, of course, meant being unnatural and guarded in their presence. Although I tried to accede to this training, I am not comfortable with that kind of dissembling. Deception is difficult for me to pull off anyway, because my actual feelings are easily read in my facial expressions.

Being married to Art and having more interactions with white people in my social life, I was learning that white folks were not as powerful and perfect as I had been led to believe. I was no longer reluctant to "offend" them, or looking for their acceptance. I had stopped straightening my hair, and started wrapping colorful scarves around my head as similar to a traditional Nigerian gelé as I could make them. When Art and I arrived at the holiday party, Vince, another assistant professor, greeted us.

"Hi Art, and hello to you too, Aunt Jemima."

Art and a few others began to laugh, but the laughter stopped abruptly when people saw my face. The room was completely silent when I replied.

"Thank you, Vince for revealing yourself. I always knew you were a racist."

Somebody gasped audibly, but Art quickly said to Vince, "She didn't mean that." Then he turned to me and in a fierce voice said, "He was joking."

Vince's wife, Beverly, entered the room and was told what happened. She walked straight up to her husband and yelled at him, "Vince, how could you say something like that? You *know* better!" Then she turned to me, "Janet, I am so sorry. So very sorry. I cannot imagine why he ..."

Before Beverly could finish, Art interrupted to chastise me, "How could you insult Vince like that? You know he's not a racist. Apologize to him!"

"I only know what I see, and he just showed me who he is. Vince knows my name. And if the two of you knew as much about black folk as you *think* you do, you'd know that what he said to me is pejorative. Period!"

My suspicions about the patronizing racism of so-called liberals were continually being confirmed. Vince and Art were good friends and we had socialized with him and Beverly, but after that night I wouldn't have anything to do with Vince. Art thought I was being wildly unreasonable because he was certain Vince's "joke" was not meant as a racist slur. Art was unable, or unwilling, to see it from my point of view; yet another indication that our marriage was done for.

I still don't understand why *anybody* believes they can or should decide for someone else what and who is offensive and/or racist.

Despite Art's obtuseness, I continued to find joy in my work. I recommended that the English Department invite Ekwueme Michael Thelwell to campus as a writer-in-residence. He came during the Winter quarter of 1968-69. I was familiar with Mike's work because his brother Richard had told me about it, and I then read his short stories. Mike initially came to the U.S. from Jamaica to study at Howard University. He was also an active member of the Student Non-Violent Coordinating Committee (SNCC/ Snick) along with better-known figures like Carmichael and Julian Bond. While Mike was in Athens, he asked us to drive him to a nearby town where Bond was speaking. Afterwards, we went out for drinks. I was excited to meet Bond, and eager to talk to him. He and Mike hadn't seen each other for a long time, and were so engrossed in catching up with each other, they forgot Art and I were there. Julian and I met again several years later and became friends.

The following academic year Mike became the founding chairman of the Department of Afro-American Studies at the University of Massachusetts, Amherst, and has been a member of their faculty since then. When I told Mike I was leaving Art, he invited me to come to UMass for graduate study. I seriously considered his offer, until I received an opportunity in California that I could not refuse.

Chapter 9

A Real Tragedy

Real tragedy is never resolved. It goes on hopelessly forever.

~ Chinua Achebe in *No Longer at Ease*

On an October evening I received a call from home telling me my younger brother Reginald and his wife Bonita were in the hospital after a fire in their home. I arranged to fly to Indianapolis right away. There, I learned more about the worst tragedy our family ever experienced.

I will never forget what Reggie told me about that night. Bonnie was planning a family party to celebrate her mother-in-law's October 26th birthday. She was to host it in the basement of their home. For fastidious Bonnie, the paint on the basement's concrete floor needed to be removed and a fresh coat applied for the occasion. She got down on her hands and knees, and using paint thinner, began scrubbing away the old paint. Reggie was upstairs watching a football game that he didn't want to leave. Bonnie called him repeatedly to come down and help. Finally, he came down, wearing thick socks and cloth house slippers. He thought it would go faster if he used a mop to spread the thinner. A while later, the pilot light on the water heater ignited. Everywhere the paint thin-

Wedding photo: Bonnie's parents, Reggie, Bonnie and my parents

ner had been applied burst into flames. Bonnie's clothes, having absorbed fumes from the thinner for over an hour, caught fire. Reggie's mop, slippers and socks were on fire as well. In a panic, Bonnie, screaming, fled up the steps, fanning the flames. Reggie yelled at her not to run and tried to stop her. By the time he caught her, Bonnie was outside the door at the top of the stairs, a human torch. Reggie pressed his body against hers and wrapped her in his arms to smother the flames. The fire did not spread beyond the basement and their two-year-old daughter, Regina, remained sound asleep in her bed. Reggie asked their neighbor, who had come outside when she heard the commotion, to go inside and get Regina. My parents came later and took Regina home with them. Reggie and Bonnie were rushed by ambulance to a hospital burn unit.

Reggie, a former U.S. Army Military Police Officer experienced in responding to trauma, talked to Bonnie

Bonnie and Regina celebrating her first birthday.

continuously to keep her from going into shock. Despite the searing pain, she remained conscious on the ride to the hospital. Hospital staff informed us that Bonnie had third degree burns over ninety percent of her body. They also said she would not live more than two or three days. Physically, Reggie fared much better. The thick socks saved his feet from deep burns. His hands and arms were more severely burned from his efforts to put out Bonnie's flames.

When I arrived, Reggie was out of the burn unit, but Bonnie was in the unit's intensive care. Only family, two at a time, could visit her for short periods. She had no skin on the only part of her body I could see: her face, neck, and arms. These visible parts were covered in what appeared to be a thick yellow ointment, possibly to ease the pain. Or, maybe that was the color of her skinless flesh; I didn't ask. She told Reggie she couldn't die because her daughter was only two, and she hadn't yet flown on an airplane. The hospital staff couldn't believe she was still alive five days later, but we were warned to expect her demise any minute. After a week, doctors started discussing what options they had for skin grafts because she had so little viable skin left.

Bonnie's will to live was formidable. For sixteen days, she refused to give up, and she was lucid until the last couple of days. My mother couldn't bear to see her in that condition, but I visited regularly. On my final visit, Bonnie was no longer conscious, and her breathing was louder than usual. When I told Mama about her noisy breathing, she said that was the "death rattle." Bonnie died that night, November 11, 1968. She was twenty-eight.

The fire department told Reggie that if the basement window had been opened even a crack, the paint thinner fumes could have escaped. Without any ventilation, sufficient fumes accumulated to be ignited by the pilot light. From that day forward, I have been conscious of having an open window, if only slightly, wherever I am. There is *always* a window open in my home, and whenever possible I open windows in other people's houses, hotel rooms, cars, and on buses. I can't open airplane windows, but wish I could!

When Reggie was released from the hospital, we both stayed at our parents' home in our old bedrooms. Reggie couldn't believe what was happening. Just days before, he had been a typical young man, happily married with a daughter. He and his wife both had jobs they liked. A year earlier they had bought a home and were looking forward to a good life together. Suddenly, a fluke fire, and he was waiting for his wife to die. The night they called to say Bonnie had breathed her last, Reggie's sorrow overwhelmed him. Mama held him in her arms while he wailed and sobbed. I sat beside him and stroked his back. Daddy quoted what he hoped were comforting words from the Bible.

After a while, through his tears Reggie mumbled, "I'm sorry, Daddy, I know I'm not being a man about this."

Daddy's response was emphatic, "Don't be sorry! If you can't cry at a time like this, there's somethin' wrong with you."

Nothing in Bonnie and Reggie's house had caught fire,

but they had lots of smoke damage. Their homeowner's insurance covered the cost of painting the entire house and having the house and all their clothes cleaned. Reggie was unable to drive because his hands and feet were still bandaged. When his house was ready, I drove him home, stayed to help with meals, driving, and whatever else he required. Plus, I didn't want him to be alone. Reggie couldn't hold a phone, and didn't really want to talk to the mortician, so I made Bonnie's funeral arrangements according to his wishes.

A day or two after we were back in the house, Bonnie's sister Brenda stopped by. We were still organizing the funeral and burial, but she wasn't there to help. Brenda charged into the bedroom and began rifling through their closet. Without explanation or asking permission, she went through Bonnie's clothes and took what she wanted. Reggie was so upset that he left his bedroom and went to sit in the kitchen. Bonnie had lots of clothes, having been a fashionable dresser who paid attention to her appearance. She was always neatly and appropriately dressed for every occasion. I was appalled that Brenda was searching through her sister's clothes and jewelry so soon after Bonnie died.

After Brenda left, I called my sister, Rosie, to express my outrage at Brenda's callous behavior. Rosie's response was to rush right over to see what she could find before Brenda took everything! Why my sister was interested in clothes that couldn't possibly fit her, I don't know, but she gathered up several things anyway. Reggie was distraught and certainly not ready to watch people walking away with his wife's personal belongings, but neither Rosie or Brenda consulted him. Reggie was not up to confronting them, so I asked Rosie if she would wait a while before taking any of Bonnie's things. She responded by accusing me of wanting

Bonnie's belongings for myself.

That was my first experience witnessing what appears to be acquisitive "grieving" after someone dies. Over the years, I've observed it many times.

Once Bonnie's obituary and funeral announcement were in the newspaper, Reggie began to receive telephone calls from women. Two of his callers were former girl-friends. Another was from a woman he knew only slightly. I was answering the telephone, and was often asked to identify myself. I'd usually hear a sigh of relief when I told them I was his sister. Reggie said these women were offering to do whatever he needed, whenever he needed it—cooking, cleaning, laundry, anything ....

I don't remember how long I was in Indianapolis, but I it must have been three weeks or more. Or perhaps I came and went on the days I didn't teach; my classes met only two days a week. Despite Art's penchant for having me nearby, he did not complain about the time I spent with my brother. It seems out of character that Art did not visit while I was in Indianapolis. Nor do I remember him attending Bonnie's funeral. Maybe he was enjoying the respite from our strained exchanges. Or possibly he was preoccupied with something or someone. I was so absorbed with the trauma and assisting Reggie that I didn't think much about his absence.

While I was in my hometown, I called Holsey, my first husband. He was in school completing his bachelor's de-gree and was still single. I wanted to see him because I was in dire need of sexual healing. Art's perpetual impotence had ended all possibility of sexual intercourse in our mar-riage, so it didn't feel like I was "cheating." Holsey willingly obliged me. I don't know if Holsey ever told anyone about our tryst, but I didn't, until now.

Reggie's grief was perhaps mitigated a bit by the generous payouts of Bonnie's life insurance policies. She had two or three of them, all of which paid double for an accidental death. In addition, Regina would receive social security survivor benefits monthly, until she turned eighteen. I could see that Reggie was not at peace, and possibly still in shock. So far as I know, he didn't receive any counseling, or unload on anyone about the impact the tragedy had on him. He never talked to me about it. When I asked how he was dealing with it, he'd shrug and say something like, "The Lord doesn't put more on us than we can bear." I suppose he had resolved to be strong and handle his ordeal like a *man!*

Not that I had been any kind of role model for Reggie of how to respond to a tragic death. My three-month-old son, Paul, had died seven years earlier, and I didn't know what to do with my grief. Instead of talking to me about taking time to grieve, nearly everyone said I should have another baby right away. Rather than examining my pain, I buried it, and ran away, hoping that a different place and new experiences would erase the memories. Instead, the unacknowledged pain took up residence in my body, wreaking havoc with my health. Many years later, I finally got the message: face the pain and grieve the loss.

Reggie was hospitalized about a week with some serious, but mostly minor burns, from which he fully recuperated. His survivor's remorse, however, lasted for the rest of his life. He may have eventually come to terms with it, if Bonnie's family had sympathized with him, but for decades his mother-in-law shunned him. She was convinced that Bonnie's death was his fault. In her grief, she apparently needed someone to blame, and since Reggie was on the scene, yet still alive, he was that someone.

Regina, Reggie's two-year-old daughter, lived with my parents while Reggie recovered, and after he returned to work. Reggie took her home with him on the weekends. She was a smart, happy, talkative little girl, and my parents were delighted to have her. They were in their sixties then, so I'm sure they welcomed the weekend respites, as well. Like all toddlers, Regina was active and required lots of attention. After a year or so of this arrangement, Mama started in on Reggie.

"You need to get married and make a home for this child."

"Not yet Ma. I'm not ready." Reggie's response was always the same. He seemed restless and determined to be rid of the insurance money as fast as possible. He seemed to be avoiding his grief by buying expensive cars, and wining and dining a series of women.

In her usual relentless style, my mother badgered Reggie about getting married. Finally, he, as I had done many times, surrendered and did what she wanted.

On a trip to Chicago, Reggie met "Patty," a savvy, attractive woman, who had a son about Regina's age. Her child was being raised by her aunt and uncle, but she was willing to take him back, and eager to move to Indianapolis with this big spender. Reggie longed for a son, so this was perfect! Mama would be pleased that he was making a home for Regina. And he and Patty would have a model family with two children, a girl and a boy. They surpassed me and Art in the speed with which they got married. By then, Regina was a charming, extremely smart four-year-old. At a family dinner to celebrate their marriage, we all heard Patty say how much she was looking forward to Mama taking "these brats" off her hands. Patty was a working woman who didn't have time for children. She must

Regina happily playing.

have been keenly disappointed to learn that Mama was giving up childcare, and that Reggie had spun a vision of a model family.

During the ten years of their marriage, Reggie relished hanging out with his son, and they spent a lot of time together. Regina was an adult when she told me that whenever Reggie and her brother went out, Patty would quickly dress and leave to do *her thing*. Regina spent lots and lots of time home alone. She began to shut down. Other family members, including Bonnie's family, were not allowed to take Regina home for a visit, unless they also took her stepbrother.

I was in town for Regina's eleventh birthday and decided to take her out to celebrate. When I picked her up, I was told her brother had to come with us. I stopped at my parents' house to comb Regina's messy hair, and left her brother with my mom. Regina and I went shopping, she picked out a nice dress for herself, and wore it out of the store. Then we went to lunch. She was reticent at first, but gradually opened up, talked to me, and even laughed a few times. After lunch, we did some sight-seeing, then I picked up her brother, and took them back home. That night, Reggie called and lit into me for combing Regina's hair, changing her clothes, and for separating her from her brother. Patty was also on the phone and added her own outrage over my transgressions. They had previously refused to allow Regina to visit me, so this bizarre tirade ended my efforts to add some joy to Regina's childhood.

My mother and sister told Reggie that Regina was being neglected. His response was that he could take care of his family without any help from them. Reggie considered it his job to look after his son, taking him shopping and hanging out with him. It was Patty's job to buy clothes for their daughter and make sure Regina was appropriately dressed, with her hair combed. Whenever Mama and Rosie saw the family, Regina would be shabbily dressed, with her hair in disarray. They said everybody else always looked like fashion models. The only person Patty looked after was Patty.

Around age twelve, voluptuous Regina and boys discovered one another. Here was a way to get the attention she craved. Whenever Regina got pregnant, Patty made sure she had an abortion, although Regina desperately wanted a baby to love. Patty was the wicked stepmother of fairy tales; however, no prince, fairy godmother, or even her dad, came to Regina's rescue.

When he and Patty divorced, Reggie lost his son, his buddy, but he stayed in touch with him. Regina was fourteen then, and determinedly rebellious, rarely attending school. Sometime after the divorce, Reggie's employer transferred him from Indianapolis to Houston. Before he moved, Reggie called to ask a favor of me.

"Can I send Regina to live with you? Being a girl, she needs to be around a woman."

"So, if I take Regina, are you going to take Kamau?" I was a single parent striving to raise my own child alone. I had no intention of doing anything as stupid as exchanging children, but I wanted him to understand how ridiculous his request was.

He was silent for a moment, and then limply said, "I can't do that. I have to work."

"I work every day, too, Reggie."

After they moved to Texas, Regina went to Job Corps.

When she was twenty-four, Regina finally had a baby to lavish with love, and she was smitten with her. Also, during her twenties, Regina was diagnosed as bipolar and schizophrenic. Parenting her daughter alone while coping with mental illness was overwhelming. Regina asked her father if they could come stay with him for a while. Reggie, who never married again, took them in when his granddaughter was around three, and became the devoted father he couldn't bring himself to be when he was younger. For nearly twenty years, until his final illness forced him to stop, he regularly worked two jobs, *and* became a census taker, so he could provide for his daughter and granddaughter.

With her father's death, Regina lost his enabling care and support. She has been struggling since. Like many mentally ill people, she doesn't like the way her prescribed medication makes her feel and frequently stops taking it. When she's off her meds, Regina has engaged in antisocial and sometimes illegal behavior. Months have elapsed when family members have no idea where she is, or how she's doing.

A few days after Bonnie's funeral, I returned to Art and my life at Ohio University, but my family of origin never felt the same after that tragic event. Our family dynamic changed as we learned unexpected things about one another. I was astonished that my sister would rummage through her sister-in-law's things immediately after her death, without any regard for the feelings of her twin brother. Despite having repeatedly seen my mother harass her children, I didn't think she'd resort to that pitiless approach with Reggie after what he'd been through. And, never would I have imagined that Reggie would turn away and allow his daughter to be neglected. I am still baffled that he not only allowed Patty's negligence, but also defended it. Reggie said he was surprised that I came to help him and stayed until he could take care of himself. It seemed like the only thing to do, so I didn't think twice about it. He needed help to see him through a very difficult time, and I was the only sibling without children. My sister had a young child, our older brother and his wife had three children, and he was away in the military, and Reggie's child was in the care of our parents.

Another awkward energy within the family was that we learned the limits of family care and influence. We watched helplessly as Regina's personality was being altered, and as her life unraveled as she got older. Whenever one of us offered guidance, or any type of assistance that we hoped might alleviate the situation, we were rejected, first by Reggie, and later by Regina. For me, Regina is an enduring reminder of her mother's tragic death. Possibly that is why Reggie looked away for so long.

Chapter 10

Shaking the Dungeon

The very time I thought I was lost, my dungeon shook and my chains fell off.

~ from the African-American spiritual,
"Free at Last"

The Levinson's, from whom we were renting the house, would return from their sabbatical at the end of the 1968-69 academic year, so we had to find another place to live. I started reading for-rent ads in the newspaper and found a likely prospect. I called to see if it was available, and it was. When Art and I arrived to look at the place shortly after my call, we were told it had been rented.

"Since when? We just spoke to you on the telephone a little while ago and you said it was available. When did you rent it?" After our experience with Sadie in Mt. Pleasant, Art knew something was up. The man showing the apartment stammered out an excuse about not knowing that it had already been rented. Ohio University had an open housing policy, and in the past, had withdrawn university approval from several landlords for their discriminatory practices. This simply made realtors devious. They no longer admitted to being racist when they were refusing to rent to black people.

Art was incensed and complained to his colleagues about it. A few of them decided to ferret out the practitioners of housing discrimination using a familiar civil rights tactic. White OU professors with white wives would immediately follow Art and me as we checked out places listed for rent. Art and I would be told the space was no longer available for one reason or another—usually because it had just been rented to someone else. When the white couple behind us were offered the apartment, we documented the details. This information was turned over to the authorities responsible for maintaining open and equal housing in Athens. Based on the evidence we gathered, several landlords lost their university approval. The people caught in our "sting" were livid, but they could hardly contest the credibility of several upstanding *white* professors.

I didn't want to live in any of the places that were being forced to rent to us. Instead, in the summer of '69, we rented an apartment in a four-unit building on Clark's Chapel Road on the edge of Athens. The owner of that building did not discriminate against black tenants. My friend Lois told me about the availability, and we rented the second-floor unit next door to her. After Art and I moved in next door, Lois and I developed a closer friendship. Whenever I couldn't stand to occupy the same space as Art, I'd go next door and unload on Lois. She also talked to me about her relationships. We stayed connected after she left Athens in January 1970 to work at Karamu House in Cleveland, her home town.

To learn more about black history and culture, that summer I signed up for a two-week workshop on African American Studies. The course was held at Atlanta University (AU) in July, and led by Richard A. Long. Dr. Long was a Professor of English and founder of AU's new African American Studies program. The weather in Atlanta was stiflingly HOT! I had never experienced such intense heat and humidity. The air felt liquid, and our dorm rooms at Clark College were *not air conditioned*. I recall sitting on the side of my bed one night, unable to sleep. It was 85 degrees at 10 p.m. and though I was sitting still, perspiration was literally streaming down my body. I was miserable. Despite the suffocating heat, I eagerly soaked up the knowledge being offered in the workshop. Dr. Long introduced us to people like educator-activists Horace Mann Bond and Mary Church Terrell. We learned more about W.E.B. DuBois's tenure at Atlanta University. He also gave us lists of resources and some of the books he recommended became a permanent part of my library. Two weeks was not long enough, I wanted to know more, much more. Still, I was happy to get out of Atlanta.

In August, my parents came to visit. By then Mama had let go of her fears about Art being a Jew. Kevin and Michael, the middle two of my older brother James' four sons, made the trip with their grandparents. My city-bred nephews were introduced to several new activities via Art's guns, hunting, and fishing pastimes, and he took pleasure in sharing his hobbies with them. Kevin was twelve and Michael nine at the time. These many years later I asked them to share what they remembered of that visit.

MICHAEL: That is by far one of my most cherished childhood memories. [It was] my first time fishing [and I] land[ed] a six-inch plus small mouth bass on my first cast. I cut off the heads of most of the forty-plus blue gills we caught, fried and ate. [I remember] your second-floor apartment atop the mountain (well at least to the mind and eye of a child), the scenic view, and the winding road and drive to get there. I even remember a green and white decal on the inside right hand side of the windshield [of Grandpa's car] that read OHIO. The letters were arched and the "O's" were larger than the "H & I." [This was an Ohio University decal Art had given Daddy.] I remember taking my first shot with a rifle (with Kevin and Art) and even going, I believe, to Mammoth cave and seeing the stalagmites and the largest and most beautiful spider web between two trees reflecting the rays of sunlight piercing through. Also, hiking along the side of a hill on a foot path that at one point had a small gap that we had to walk over, and a footprint that over time had made its impression in the stone walkway. So, you ask, "do you remember"? I reply YES and could provide many more detailed memories.

KEVIN: My memory is not as good as Michael's, but I do recall that we went fishing and had a delicious fish fry with all the fish we caught.

Art, the boys and I prepared to clean the fish until Kevin discovered that we were cutting the heads off live fish, then pulling out their guts. That made him nauseous, so he left the kitchen and joined Mama and Daddy in the living room. Michael had no problem with it at all! On another day, we drove about an hour to Hocking Hills State Park where we hiked, then toured Old Man's Cave and Art explained the difference between stalagmites and stalactites. They are both mineral deposits that line the insides of a cave. Stalactites hang from the *ceiling* like icicles and stalagmites emerge from the *ground* and stand up like traffic cones.

Art fishing with Kevin and Michael

Art and me with the catch

Hiking Hocking Hills State Park

We all enjoyed the visit.

For the 1969-70 academic year, Art changed his teaching days from Mondays and Wednesdays to Tuesdays and Thursdays, the same days I taught. As usual, he did not discuss the change with me before he made it. He said he wanted us to spend more time together. AARGH! I couldn't believe it! Except for occasional social engagements, we were at home alone together, day and night, every Friday, Saturday, Sunday and Monday.

The togetherness did not bring us closer; rather we had explosive arguments about nearly everything. I was done being bullied and manipulated by Art into doing what he wanted regardless of how I felt. My resistance made him more determined, escalating our contentiousness. In addition, Art was drinking so much and so often that I began to wonder if he was an alcoholic. After work, he always made drinks for the two of us because *he* didn't want to drink alone. Although he probably had four drinks to my one, still I was consuming more alcohol than I ever had in my life. Our liquor-fueled bickering became so intense at times that it seemed prudent to place myself between Art and the room where he kept his guns. I thought I would get to the guns before he did, or at least slow down his access long enough for him to have second thoughts. Fortunately, he never went for a weapon; otherwise I probably wouldn't be here writing this.

I didn't yet have a precise departure date, but every time I got paid, I put my entire check into a savings account so that when I did, I would have money to begin my new life. Art's salary went into our joint checking account, and so long as I kept the bills paid, he didn't seem interested in our finances. When Art asked about our savings account, which was in my name, I told him he could add his name whenever he wanted. He didn't mention it again until the day he rushed home demanding that we go to the bank right away to add his name to our savings account. Art wanted to purchase a new gun that cost more than was available in our checking account. When he tried to make a withdrawal from "our" savings account, he couldn't. He was furious! That day my savings account became, in fact, *our* savings account. DAMN! That shook me up. I immediately opened another savings account at a different bank for my paychecks, but now that Art had seen the balance, he was itching to spend it. When he started talking about buying a farm, I was rattled. He had a habit of making such decisions without saying a word to me; I had to get away before he spent the money I had put aside.

One night during one of our heated exchanges, frustration and alcohol spurred me to scream, "If you think I'm going to put up with this crap for the rest of my life, you're out of your mind!"

"What did you say?"

"You heard me! I'm sick of this shit. This little town with no black people. And now you're talking about buying a farm out in the country somewhere where we'll be even more isolated!? No way am I going for that!" I didn't include his impotence as one other thing I was fed up with; that issue died so long ago, it wasn't worth mentioning.

Art was incredulous, "Are you serious? You want to leave? All this time you've *used* me, and now you…."

It was my turn to be astounded. Did he say, *I used him*?! Unbelievable! *I used him*? Really? I was livid! I thought of backhanding him hard enough to make him spin, but I knew a better way. In a calm, deliberate voice, I said, "You racist mothafucka! What the fuck makes you think you brought more to this relationship than I did?"

He looked as if I *had* slapped him. Art didn't say anything, but his eyes glistened with tears. After all, he was a political radical, a Marxist, former president of the campus NAACP, active member of CORE, and he had capped it all off by marrying a black woman. How could he possibly be racist?

Neither of us had anything to say for the remainder of that night.

I immediately regretted having alerted him that I planned to leave, but it didn't seem to matter. Either he assumed I was speaking in a moment of rage, or he didn't believe I had the moxie to go off on my own. We remained in the sham that was our marriage for several more weeks, without ever referring to the night I cursed him. During those interminable weekends with Art, I buried myself in grading papers and preparing for my classes. When I wasn't working, I'd read a book. He said I read to shut him out; he preferred that we watch television *together*. By the time Tuesday morning arrived, every cell in my body was straining to be away from him. He, on the other hand, wanted to extend our time together by having lunch on campus. Not only had he changed the days he taught, but he'd also arranged his class times to coincide with mine. I know he felt my alienation, but I was amiable because I didn't want him to suspect what I was up to. The fact that we weren't physically intimate, made being genial easier.

Art's desire to control my every movement and moment had a lot to do with his need for constant companionship. He despised being alone. He told me he got married so he'd always have someone to do things with. I don't think it ever occurred to him that I could have preferences of my own, or if I did, that they should be considered. I laughed out loud, the first time Art said he wanted me to go hunting and fishing with him. I went fishing a couple of times, but I wasn't about to go off in the woods with Art carrying guns. He had insisted on teaching me how to shoot a rifle, a shotgun, and a .38 handgun. He gave me a .22 caliber pistol for a birthday present, even though he knew I didn't like guns. I had it for years, but never used it. Why would I? I was never comfortable with a gun in my home, and finally got rid of it.

A second black faculty member was hired that academic year to join Jim Barnes in the political science department. Lillian Ramos was a fiftyish attorney from Cleveland who was popular with students. Perhaps because she was older, when she spoke to students, they listened. I was grateful to hear her blast them for their lack of interest in their history. She said they couldn't be viable "revolutionaries" if they didn't know anything about those who had paved the way for them. Art and I were getting to know Dr. Ramos, and were among a group she invited to a holiday dinner at her house during the winter break. Early in January she and I were among those who participated in a Teach-In on the life and work of Martin Luther King Jr. I talked about King's "final testament," *The Trumpet of Conscience,* published in 1968, and based on speeches King delivered in Canada in 1967. I remember that she complimented me on my presentation. By the end of the month Ramos was dead of a massive coronary occlusion. She had been at OU a mere five months, but left a lasting impression. The Lillian Ramos Award is presented each year to the outstanding African American Political Science major. It is funded by contributions from faculty, colleagues, and students.

A new graduate student enrolled at OU that fall as well. He was married and said he was a member of the Nation of Islam. He went by the name Alton X. Although he was nearly ten years older than the undergraduate activists, he became enthusiastically involved with them. Because he was older and a member of the Nation, the student leaders respected him and listened to his advice. One night when I stopped at a gas station to fill up our car, one of my students, whom I knew well, got out of a car full of black males. He approached me carrying a red metal gas can saying his car had run out of gas and he needed money to fill the can. I often helped students, so I used my credit card to fill his can. I saw Alton X watching us from the back-seat window. That same night a university building caught fire. It was unclear if the fire had been deliberately set. There was speculation around campus that black student activists had burned the building to underscore their demands for a Black Studies program.

In the summer of 1969, Claude Sowle had replaced Vernon Alden as president. When Art and I attended a faculty reception for him, Dr. Sowle quietly asked me if I had set fire to that building. I was jolted by his question and responded emphatically that I had not. Why did he ask me that!? Probably because he'd been told I was a fervent supporter of the students' demonstrations and demands. But still, that was a startling bit of cocktail banter. After thinking long and hard about his peculiar question, I remembered the gas can I had filled with my credit card. Once I had connected the two events, I told Art. He was gleeful that we may have assisted students in "a revolutionary act." He was not concerned about Sowle's inquiry, because he said, "If they really suspected you of being involved, you would have been arrested." I never heard any more about it.

Many years later, I ran into a man who had been a faculty member at OU the same time I was there. He told me that Alton X had been dispatched to OU by COIN-

TELPRO, the FBI's program to infiltrate and disrupt black political activity. Like so many other FBI plants in organizations created to change the status quo of our oppression, Alton's assignment was to be an *agent provocateur*. These provocateurs induced unsuspecting activists to engage in violent and unlawful activities to expose them to crackdowns, arrests, or worse by authorities. When I heard that, I remembered that Alton X had been in the car with the students on the night I filled the gas can. I concluded that if they had indeed burned the building, it was his idea. That former faculty member also said that Alton continued his work for the FBI after he left OU, and had been found shot to death on the street in New York City. I don't know if any of this is true, but it seems plausible.

That fall, another opportunity to learn more about African American history and literature was again being offered by Dr. Long. A Black Studies conference, directed by him was held in a hotel in Atlanta. Since the conference was in November, I figured I'd be safe from Atlanta's heat. Art thought I should go with him to Arizona where he was presenting a paper to an anthropology conference that same weekend. But it was when he told me about his paper, that I started looking for professional possibilities I could participate in at the same time. I wanted to learn as much as I could, but I was equally interested in finding a lover. I hadn't had sex for over a year!

I could barely think of anything except getting laid! I had grown up in a nurturing home, but one without affection. Physical contact was verboten; we didn't even hug one another! I longed to be touched and held. Once I discovered the intimate touch and closeness I craved could be had with sex, I couldn't get enough. For me, the primary allure of marriage was that it promised regular sexual intimacy. It never occurred to me that my husband would lose interest in sex. Or, if Art had a sexual appetite, it wasn't for me.

A welcome-to-the-conference cocktail party was held for registrants on the first night. I swept the room with my eyes and saw a handsome black man standing alone with a drink in his hand. I walked over and introduced myself. I learned that "Guy" was an assistant professor at Bowie State College (now university), in Maryland. He lived in Washington, D.C. with his wife. Like us, they had no children. The attraction was mutual. Guy and I spent most of the weekend together. I had a lot of catching up to do, and apparently, so did he. We also managed to attend conference sessions.

I was so sore when I returned home, I had to see a physician. After he examined me, he wrote a prescription to treat a bladder infection. With a big grin, he told me my condition was sometimes called "honeymoonitis," and recommended that my husband and I refrain from sex for a couple of weeks. Ha! That would be easy. I was a little uneasy, though, about how Art might react to my diagnosis.

"What did the doctor say?"

"He said I have a bladder infection."

"What do you do for a bladder infection?

"I have a prescription that should clear it up in a couple of weeks."

"Well, take it easy. I don't want you to be sick."

Wow! That's all he has to say!

That response was so tepid, I had a disturbing thought: Art knows why I'm in pain, but he's willing to accept it, so long as our marriage remains intact.

Guy and I kept in touch. My friend, Lois, by then Executive Director at Cleveland's Karamu House, invited me to be a member of the Karamu Arts Advisory Board. When I attended the board's occasional meetings, Guy would meet me in Cleveland. Interestingly, Art never asked to go with me for those meetings.

In my second year with the English department, they doubled their black faculty by hiring Quincy Troupe, a published poet from Los Angeles. OU was his first teaching job as well. Quincy and I were about the same age, shared common interests in literature and politics, and became allies. When the English Department sent out an announcement about their annual poetry series, Quincy and I had the same reaction when we saw the list of poets. They were all white males! When we pointed that out to the department chairman, he seemed genuinely surprised that we were questioning the list, but asked what we suggested.

Quincy and I proposed an African American poetry series to balance their "traditional" poetry series. The English Department supported our proposal. Consequently, several black poets visited, one at a time, during the Fall and Winter quarters. Each poet read and discussed their work at a public lecture, then came to the poetry classes that Quincy and I were teaching and talked to the students about the craft of writing poetry. The poets included emerging writers who were not yet well-known, like Jayne Cortez and Robert Chrisman, as well as acclaimed, award-winning poets like Mari Evans and Robert Hayden.

Chrisman was also editor of *The Black Scholar,* a newly minted monthly "Journal of Black Studies and Research" featuring politically-inclined scholarly articles about African people throughout the diaspora. Chrisman was impressed with my efficiency in planning and organizing the series and arranging his travel and accommodations. He showed me the first issue of *The Black Scholar* and asked if I would be interested in working for them. They needed someone to read submissions and help edit the articles selected for publication. What an exciting opportunity: I could be part of an innovative publication that was on the cutting-edge of the black studies movement. The journal looked impressive and had an illustrious board of contributing and advisory editors that included an array of accomplished and well known blacks, including historian Lerone Bennett of *Ebony* magazine; Ossie Davis, actor and playwright; Joyce Ladner, Institute of the Black World; poet Sonia Sanchez; and James Turner, Director of Africana Studies at Cornell University, and Art's former student at CMU.

I was awed when I saw that Nathan Hare, the activist professor mentioned above, was the publisher. Hare was an icon among young blacks for his uncompromising advocacy for the study and teaching of black history and culture. It would be sensational to not only have a job waiting when I exited my marriage, but to work with Dr. Hare was especially thrilling! After he left Howard, Hare joined the faculty at California State University, San Francisco (SF State) where Chrisman also taught. They were both fired for organizing students to demand that SF State establish ethnic studies programs. Chrisman knew Allan Ross, a Russian Marxist émigré and successful printer whose business was in Sausalito, at the other end of San Francisco's Golden Gate Bridge. It was vital that Chrisman and Ross have a high-profile African American with impeccable credentials to help launch the journal. And the twice fired Dr. Hare would have a platform for his black studies crusade. It was a good fit. Office space was set up at Ross' printing operation, and the three of them started *The Black Scholar*, which was financed and printed by Ross.

It was time for me to make my move. In fact, it had become urgent because Art was actively looking for property to buy. He was scheduled to attend an anthropology conference in April, so that became the target date for my departure. The conference was between the Winter and Spring quarters so I knew he'd want me to go with him. Before he could ask, I told him I had promised to visit my widowed brother, Reggie, during the break. Instead, I informed the department chair I was resigning effective at the end of Winter quarter. I called my brothers, asked them to rent a U-Haul trailer, and told them when to come pick me up.

My brothers were surprised I was leaving Art, because I had not talked to anybody about my plans except Lois. I didn't want to become campus gossip, but more important, I was ashamed. No one in my immediate family had ever been divorced, yet here I was leaving my *second* husband! On the ride to Indianapolis, James wanted to know what happened.

"We haven't had sex in a couple of years."

"WHAT?! Are you kidding me?" He was shocked.

Reggie turned around in his seat and looked at me, as if he was expecting to see laughter, because surely, I had to be joking! Then, he said, "I'm surprised you stayed as long as you did."

Explanation sufficient! We talked about other things.

It was not that simple with my parents. I told them Art was planning to buy a farm and I didn't want to be stuck out in the country for the rest of my life. I focused on how thrilled I was about the wonderful opportunity in California. For my family, my moving away from home, plus marrying Art had tagged me as "different;" they were learning to accept the unexpected from me. The fact that I was about to move to California, alone, was just more evidence of my eccentricity. Mama didn't even try to talk me out of it.

Guy knew I was leaving and asked me to come to D.C. He was sure with his connections, I could get a job there. I didn't even consider that. He became angry when I told him I already had a job in California and was moving there. For some reason, he thought I should have checked with him

SEPTEMBER 1970 $1.25

THE**BLACK**SCHOLAR

BLACK STUDIES

ANDERSON
BANKS
DU BOIS
JAMES
SUNDIATA

before I made plans. His reaction simply underscored the wisdom of my choice. Being Guy's secret mistress in D.C. would simply trade one galling relationship for another. I meant to be free.

The invitation from Mike Thelwell to do graduate work at UMass was more difficult to turn down, because I wanted more education, but my heart was pulling me west. Since childhood I had longed to be a writer and editor, but didn't know how to gain entrée to that world. Working for *The Black Scholar* would be that entrée. My dream was complete when an article I wrote was published in the May 1970 issue of *The Black Scholar*.

I drove Art to the airport in Columbus. He thought I would keep driving west to Indianapolis, but I went back

THE **BLACK** SCHOLAR

Journal of Black Studies and Research

The Black Scholar staff and advisory editors

to Athens to pack for the move. I was only taking personal stuff—my clothing, books, the first piece of original art I purchased, and the money from the savings accounts. I had purchased duplicates of items we both used—IBM Selectric typewriter, portable tape recorder, reference books—and stored them in my office cubicle at the English Department. I left Art a note saying he was welcome to keep our tax refund. I did not tell him where I was going. We had been married four years and four months.

I called him at the conference hotel. "Art, I've moved out, so you need to find someone to pick you up at the airport when you come home. I won't be there."

"What are you talking about?"

"I've left. Our marriage is over. I've moved out."

"You *can't leave*. We have to talk about this. Where are you?"

"I'm at Reggie's right now, temporarily."

"Janet, come back. You can't do this! We can work this out."

"I'm not coming back."

He called my parents and my brother a few times looking for me. Reggie finally told Art I wasn't in Indianapolis, but he did not tell him where I was.

After a few weeks passed, someone reading *The Black Scholar* saw that I was associate editor and told Art. He called me at the office and again asked if we could talk about reviving our marriage. He even volunteered for the first time, ever, to talk about our sex life, but I was done.

In San Francisco, I stayed with Chrisman and his wife (and also rode to work with him) until I found an apartment. It took only a few days. The place I rented was expensive, a $145-a-month, third-floor walk-up! The location however, was ideal and an easy commute for my daily drive to Sausalito. Everything else I needed—laundromat, grocery store, restaurants—was within walking distance. The apartment was on Stanyan Street near Frederick, overlooking Kezar Stadium in Golden Gate Park. The couple moving out of the apartment had a single bed, a small kitchen table and two chairs they didn't want. I asked them to leave the items for me, since I had no furniture.

I loved the Haight-Ashbury neighborhood. I bought a new red Ford Maverick to drive to work. I'd never lived in a major city, yet San Francisco felt like HOME! I loved it. I reveled in walking down the street hearing other languages being spoken and seeing such a variety of people. San Franciscans were friendly and eager to show me their city. I visited neighborhoods that replicated cultures from different parts of the world, and was introduced to new, delicious foods—eating sushi for the first time. The weather was not as warm as I had expected; I had foolishly given my winter coat to my sister before I left. In the mornings when I left my apartment in the Haight to go to work, the cool moist air required at least a jacket, and sometimes a coat. But after a glorious drive across the Golden Gate Bridge, I removed my outer layer because Sausalito was sunny and warm.

Epilogue

I lived in the San Francisco Bay Area for three and a half productive years. After a brief stint with *The Black Scholar*, I enrolled in graduate courses in American Literature at Cal State, Hayward, and later in the English doctoral program at Stanford University. I also taught composition and African American literature at Foothill College. Most significantly, with soul mate Walter Bell, I had a magnificent son, W. Kamau Bell. Eight months after Kamau was born, my father died. Mama was at a loss without Daddy, and we needed someone to care for Kamau when I returned to work, so we moved to Indianapolis. Just before his sixth birthday, Kamau and I moved to Boston where I began my dream job as a book editor.

Although Art and I had a couple of telephone conversations, we never saw each other again. He purchased a farm shortly after I left, and remarried in 1972. He remained married, residing on his farm, and at Ohio University until he died in 1998 at age sixty-three.

For more of my excellent adventures, see my essay collection, *Not All Poor People Are Black,* and my son's book, *The Awkward Thoughts of W. Kamau Bell.*

Notes

CHAPTER 1 **Going to War**

6   Along with the nearby towns of Bay City: Saginaw City Directory, 1964

6   Martha Ludwick, the woman looking: Michigan Civil Rights Commission complaint #618–Hsg, filed 1/20/65

10   He's helped it as much as Abraham Lincoln.": *American Legacy*, Fall 2007, p. 41

14   playing the dozens: verbal combat, played mostly by black males, in which the participants insult each other's relatives, especially their mothers.

CHAPTER 2 **Being Called to Struggle**

19   not to bother to send the money": *The Saginaw News*, February 19, 1965

20   "long, rancorous discussion: *ibid.*

21   "This hypocrite is going to get blasted: *The Messenger: The Rise and Fall of Elijah Muhammad* by Karl Evanzz, 1999

22   Dr. Alvin Loving: *Leaders in Education*, R.R. Bowker, 5th edition, 1974

28   500 tickets sold: *Indianapolis Recorder,* July 24, 1965

28   "Clergymen Face Test: *The Saginaw News*, February 28, 1965

CHAPTER 3 **Needing a Change**

42   "To the ordinary American or Englishman: Quoted in *When and Where I Enter* by Paula Giddings, 1986

43   The *plaçage: We Are Your Sisters*, edited by Dorothy Sterling, 1984

44   Essie Mae Washington-Williams: *Dear Senator: A Memoir by the Daughter of Strom Thurmond*, 2005.

44   Indiana legalized: *The History of Indiana Law* by David J. Bodenhamer, Randall T. Shepard

45   number has risen to seventeen percent: "Interracial Marriage in America is the Highest It's Ever Been Since Loving *v* Virginia," by Janice Williams in *Newsweek*, May 18, 2017

48   committed suicide: https://web.archive.org/ web/20061026084532/http://susiebright.blogs.com/ susie_brights_journal_/2006/10/checking_out.html

CHAPTER 4 **Listening for the Sound of the Genuine**

54   Sadie Higgins: listed as the owner at this address in the 1966 Mt. Pleasant City Directory.

88   To cover his expenses: *Ohio University 1804-2004:*
      The Spirit of a Singular Place by Betty Hollow, 2003

CHAPTER 7 **Making Demands**

101   "one drop" rule: http://news.harvard.edu/gazette/
      story/2010/12/one-drop-rule-persists/

104   National Advisory Commission on Civil Disorders:
      http://www.history.com/this-day-in-history/kerner-
      commission-report-released

104   The FBI's COINTELPRO: https://www.noi.org/coin-
      telpro/

106   "Strong Men" excerpt: *The Collected Poems of Sterling*
      A. Brown selected by Michael S. Harper, 1980.

107   about 4,000 of us: *Speaking for Myself* by Vernon R.
      Alden, 1997.

107   "Like a true king: *Ohio University Alumnus,* June-
      July 1968

107   "two hundred grieving students: Hollow, *op.cit.*

108   Negro History Week: *Ohio University Alumnus,* May-
      June 1968.

108   "There were more African American: Betty Hollow
      in *A Conversation about Ohio University and the*
      Presidency by Charles Ping, 2014

108 "A Hand is on the Gate": Interview with Lois Mc-
     Guire.

109 graduated its first black: Alden, *op.cit.*

109 "satisfactory housing": *ibid.*

111 Viola Liuzzo: http://www.biography.com/people/
     viola-gregg-liuzzo-370152

111 Andrew Goodman: http://www.core-online.org/His-
     tory/goodman.htm

111 Michael Schwerner: http://www.core-online.org/His-
     tory/schwerner.htm

113 "Black students at Ohio University: Alden, *op.cit.*

114 "My life and that of: *Life and Death in the Central
     Highlands* by James T. Gillam and Allan R. Millett,
     2010

114 "I believe the University: *Ohio University Alumnus,*
     June-July 1968

114 "The mood of the campus: Hollow, *op.cit.*

114 "[There was] sharp, often savage: Alden, *op.cit.*

116 "Alden led the University: http://ohiofellows.net/His-
     tory.php

CHAPTER 8 **Choosing New Possibilities**

CHAPTER 10 **Shaking the Dungeon**

Acknowledgments

I am grateful to my late cousin, Alma Johnson Civils and her daughters, Portia and Marcia, for taking care of me while I was in Lansing doing research at the Library of Michigan.

Leo Lefevre, of the Saginaw Public Library's Local History and Genealogy department, was kind enough to provide copies of pages from the MacArthur High School yearbooks that helped verify my memories.

My long-time friend, Lois McGuire was especially helpful with names and places in Athens, Ohio and at Ohio University (OU). My former students at OU, Michel Perdreau and Bari Teamor, also provided leads and reminders. In addition, Dr. Robin Muhammad, Chair, Department of African American Studies at OU, and her student assistant, Olivia Blackburn, delivered important research assistance that precluded my having to travel to Athens. The Monroe County (Indiana) Library, as usual, provided help when I needed it.

I am fortunate to have friends who love, support, encourage, and even rescue me when necessary. This wonderful group includes Lynne Thompson, Madeline Scales-Taylor, Vinita Ricks, Denise Owens, Audrey McCloskey, Elizabeth Mandell, Mary Sullivan Madore, Delores Logan, Merridee LaMantia, Sophia Fatouros, Tanja Bisesi, and Mildred Morgan Ball. I especially appreciate Jennifer Deam, a talented writer who provides essential feedback that helps improve my writing. I am immensely grateful to the participants in Wild at Heart (past and present) for nurturing my spiritual growth.

Thanks to my nieces and nephews— Kevin, Miguel, and Madganna, in particular—who check on me and always have my back. Above all, unending gratitude and love to those who galvanize my life: my precious granddaughters and their magnificent parents.

Index

Brown, Jim, 83, 84
Brown, Sterling, 106
Browns, Cleveland (NFL), 84, 108
Bureau of the Census, 2, 102

C

California, 21, 22, 46, 47, 48, 105, 106, 113, 126, 130, 156, 157, 158
California State University, Hayward, 126
capitalism, 60, 61, 95
Caribbean, 94, 121
Caribbean Festival of the Arts, 121
Carifesta, *see* Caribbean Festival of the Arts
Carmichael, Stokely, 21, 25, 82, 83, 85, 105, 128
cars, 5, 6, 36, 87, 138, 152, 153
Celtics, Boston (NBA), 84
Central Michigan University, 35, 55, 58, 86, 156
Charleston, West Virginia, 88
Charly (movie), 125
Cheatham, Annie (Mama), 2, 3, 4, 5, 25, 26, 34, 42, 49, 50-54, 58, 61, 67, 134, 138, 139, 140, 145, 146, 158
Cheatham, Bonita (Bonnie), 51, 131-137, 139, 142
Cheatham, Gregory Ramon, 58
Cheatham, Kevin Lamar, 145-147
Cheatham, Michael James, 145-147
Cheatham, Regina, 58, 132, 133, 137-142
Cheatham, Reginald, 50, 51, 53, 58, 131-142, 157, 159, 160, 161
Cheatham, Rosie, *see* Mickey, Rosie
Cheatham, Smith Henry (Daddy), 4, 6, 25, 26, 27-28, 49, 50, 53, 54, 58, 134, 146
   Testimonial Dinner, 27-28
Chicano, 11

Long, Richard A., 144, 145, 153
Loving, Alvin Sr., 22, 23, 24, 30
Loving *v.* Virginia, 2, 44-45
Ludwick, Martha, 6, 20

M

MacArthur High School, 1, 5, 6, 10-13, 15, 16, 18, 20, 38,
    39, 58, 76
Makeba, Miriam, 94
Malcolm X, 20, 21, 79, 82, 85, 105, 119, 120, 122
Manchild in the Promised Land (Brown), 79, 119
Manley, Michael, 121
marriage, 2, 24, 25, 34, 40, 41, 42, 44, 45, 49, 50, 51, 55, 56,
    57, 69, 76, 81, 87, 91, 92, 110, 111, 112, 121, 129, 136,
    138, 139, 150, 153, 154, 156, 159, 160
Marshall, Thurgood, 60, 72, 85
Marxism, 60
Massachusetts, 84, 101, 130
Matthews, Charles, 126
McCarthy, Eugene, 103
McClinton, Curtis, 84
McGuire, Lois, 109, 144, 154, 157
McKissick, Floyd, 108
mental illness, 141
Meriweather, Diane, 29-30
Meriweather, Jesse, 29
Miami, Florida, 36, 91-94, 97
Michigan, 1, 8, 29, 44, 45, 48, 62, 87
    Ann Arbor, 30, 31, 45, 57-59, 67, 68, 70, 76, 80, 86, 87
    Lansing, 4, 26, 58
    Ludington, 27
    Mt. Pleasant, 35-37, 40, 54, 56, 57, 86, 143
    Saginaw (*see* Saginaw, Michigan)

Oakland, California, 21,105
Obama, President Barack Hussein, 102
octoroon, 43
O'Dell, Rex, 11
Ohio University, 86-88, 108, 109, 116, 122, 126, 127, 142,
    143, 146, 152
    English Department, 109, 117, 119, 125, 130, 155, 159
    student demonstrations, 113, 114
one-drop rule, 101-102
oppression, 9, 60, 84, 96, 105, 153

P-Q
Pace *v.* Alabama, 45
Packers, Green Bay (NFL), 84
Page, Clarence, 126
Patriots, Boston (NFL), 84
Paul (deceased son), 26, 137
People's National Party
plaçage, 43
Porterfields, 9
Powell, Adam Clayton, Jr., 71-72
Primus, Pearl, 85
quadroon, 43

R
racial oppression, 9, 96, 105
racist behavior, 9, 16, 18-21, 38, 39, 55-56, 71, 76, 102, 122,
    129
Ramos, Lillian, 151
Rance, Beale, 5, 7, 22
Rance, Odahlia, 4, 5, 7, 8, 15, 22, 40
Rasta (*see* Mystic Revelation)
Red Hawks, Washington (NFL), 84

slavers, 100, 101, 102

slavery (in the United States), 43, 88, 96, 104, 119, 124

Smith, Lucy, 15-19, 28, 29, 38, 39, 45, 46

Snick (*see* Student Non-Violent Coordinating Committee)

Sowle, Claude, 152

Southern Christian Leadership Conference (SCLC), 21, 113

Spingarn, Arthur and Joel, 51

Stanford University, 127

Steele, James, 107, 114, 115,

Sterlin, Rene and Anne, 90

Stokes, Carl, 83,

"Strong Men" (Brown), 106-107

Student Non-Violent Coordinating Committee (SNCC), 21, 105, 113, 130

T-U-V

Templeton, John Newton, 88, 109

Tennessee, 4, 104, 128

Terrell, Mary Church, 145

Thelwell, Ekwueme Michael, 99, 130, 158

Thelwell, Richard, 40, 72, 73, 91, 94-99, 120, 121

TransAfrica, 57

Transatlantic Slave Trade, 43, 102

Ture, Kwame, *see* Stokely Carmichael

Turner, James, 56, 156

Tuskegee University, 88

Up from Slavery (Washington), 124

urban rebellions, 70

U.S. Congress, 9, 71, 72

U.S. Supreme Court, 1, 2, 44, 72, 85

Vietnam War, 84, 85

Vietra (family maid), 92, 93, 97
violence (*also see* guns), 20, 74, 77, 79, 80, 82, 104-107,
    111, 153

W-X-Y-Z
Wallace, Mike, 20
Walker, Margaret, 120
Washington, Booker T., 88, 124
weight, 62
white supremacy, 85, 96, 102
Whitmore Lake Boys Training School, 76
Wilkins, Roy, 84
Williams, Arlene and Ron, 91
Williams, Sid, 84
Wilson, Robert G., 88
women, 25, 39, 42, 50, 56, 68, 111, 114, 116, 118, 126, 136,
    138
  exploitation of, 12, 34, 43, 44, 69-70, 80, 102, 113
Wooten, John, 84, 108
Wright, Richard, 123
Wurtsmith Air Force Base, 22
Yerby, Frank, 123
Young, Whitney, 84

Also by JANET CHEATHAM BELL

The Time and Place That Gave Me Life
Sabayt Publications, 2016; Indiana University Press, 2007
(also available as an e-book)

*Not All Poor People Are Black and other things we need to
think more about*
Sabayt Publications, 2015 (also available as an e-book)

Victory of the Spirit: Reflections on My Journey
Sabayt Publications, 2011 (also available as an e-book)

Famous Black Quotations® on Birthdays
Andrews McMeel, 2003

Famous Black Quotations® on Love
Andrews McMeel, 2003

*Till Victory Is Won: Famous Black Quotations® from the
NAACP* Simon & Schuster, 2002 (also available as an e-book)

Famous Black Quotations® on Mothers
Andrews McMeel, 2002

Famous Black Quotations® on Sisters
Andrews McMeel, 2002

Stretch Your Wings: Famous Black Quotations® for Teens
(co-author) Little, Brown and Company, 1999

The Soul of Success: Inspiring Quotations for Entrepreneurs, John Wiley & Sons, 1997

Literature Connections Sourcebook for The Souls of Black Folk and Related Readings, McDougal Little, 1997 (work for hire)

Victory of the Spirit: Meditations on Black Quotations
Warner Books (now Grand Central Publishing), 1996

Famous Black Quotations®
Warner Books, 1995

Famous Black Quotations® on Women, Love and other topics Sabayt Publications, 1992

***Famous Black Quotations®* Calendars,** Sabayt Publications, 1988-1991

African Heritage Bibliography, Baker & Taylor, 1989

Hispanic Bibliography of the U.S., (co-author) Baker & Taylor, 1987-1989

The Black Family Reunion Cookbook, Tradery House, 1991

Famous Black Quotations® and Some Not So Famous
Sabayt Publications, 1986

"Teaching Ethnic Literature: Some Preliminary Considerations" in the *Indiana English Journal*, Indiana Council of Teachers of English, Spring 1977

"Challenging Racism and Sexism" in the *Hoosier Schoolmaster*, Indiana Department of Public Instruction, 1976

With Liberty and Justice for All (annotated bibliography), Indiana Department of Public Instruction, 1975

My Face is Full of Your Blood (sound/slide presentation), Indiana Department of Public Instruction, 1974

Teaching Black: An Evaluation of Methods and Resources (co-author) African and Afro-American Studies Program, Stanford University, 1971

"Malik El Shabazz: A Survey of His Interpreters" in *The Black Scholar*, May 1970

෨ ❖ ෫

FOR MORE ABOUT THE AUTHOR
please see
www.janetcheathambell.com

෨ ❖ ෫

Made in the USA
Lexington, KY
10 September 2018